HOW CHINA SEES THE WORLD

For Karl —

Your aunt Ellie and I are so proud of you. Someday we will be really your book

Uncle Bradley

How China Sees the World

HAN-CENTRISM AND THE
BALANCE OF POWER IN
INTERNATIONAL POLITICS

John M. Friend and Bradley A. Thayer

POTOMAC BOOKS | *An imprint of the University of Nebraska Press*

All rights reserved. Potomac Books is an
imprint of the University of Nebraska Press.
Manufactured in the United States of America.

Library of Congress Cataloging-in-Publication Data
Names: Friend, John M., author. |
Thayer, Bradley A., author.
Title: How China sees the world: Han-
centrism and the balance of power in
international politics / John M.
Friend and Bradley A. Thayer.
Description: Lincoln: Potomac Books,
An imprint of the University of
Nebraska Press, 2018. | Includes
bibliographical references and index.
Identifiers: LCCN 2018027389
ISBN 9781612349831 (hardback)
ISBN 9781640121355 (epub)
ISBN 9781640121362 (mobi)
Subjects: LCSH: China—Foreign relations—
21st century. | Nationalism—China.
| National characteristics, Chinese. |
China—Ethnic relations. | BISAC:
political science / Political Ideologies / Nationalism.
Classification: LCC JZ1734 .F75 2018 |
DDC 327.51—dc23
LC record available at https://lccn.loc.gov/2018027389.

Set in Adobe Garamond by Mikala R. Kolander.
Designed by N. Putens.

This book is dedicated to

Andrew W. Marshall

a foremost U.S. strategist during the Cold War and afterward,

in honor of the contributions he made to the security of the United States and its allies and to the advancement of strategic thought in the U.S. Department of Defense and national security community.

CONTENTS

TABLES

ACKNOWLEDGMENTS

Many individuals made time to answer our questions about China and to provide context concerning how the Chinese envision national identity and nationalism. John F. Copper, the Stanley J. Buckman Distinguished Professor of International Studies at Rhodes College, discussed with us his theory of how the Chinese perceive both their nation and how their leaders see the world, and he was a great aid to us when he shared his thoughts regarding how the Chinese see the United States and its vulnerabilities.

Professor Eric Hyer of Brigham Young University was of great assistance as we discussed China's concept of national identity, race, racial differences, and how their outlook affects their view of the United States. Professor David Mungello of the Department of History at Baylor University also was a great help to us in numerous discussions about the Chinese worldview, the Chinese attitude toward racial and religious minorities, particularly their perspectives on Christians, and their perception of the United States, Europe, India, and Russia. Professors Huiyun Feng and Kai He, both of Griffith University, aided us time and again with translations, broadening our understanding of Chinese foreign policy and motivations, China's concept of strategy, and of *shi* [势], while permitting us to comprehend how ancient many of these beliefs are, how they were woven into Chinese history and culture, and why they remain.

Thayer presented a draft of the argument at the International Relations Research Colloquium of the Department of Politics and International Relations at the University of Oxford. He is grateful to the conveners, Professor Dominic Johnson and Dr. Nicole de Silva for the opportunity to present and to Paola Solimena (DPIR) for her critique, as well as to the participants for their exceptional comments and suggestions. In addition, Thayer thanks Ólafur Darri Björnsson for his efficient and indefatigable research assistance. He is grateful to the staff at the Longwall Library at Magdalen College, University of Oxford, especially Daryl Green and Maggie Wainwright, the Social Science Library, University of Oxford, and the Bodleian Library for their assistance locating sources. At the Bodleian, he is grateful for the hospitality of the Upper Reading Room and Duke Humfrey's Library, in particular, which was a wonderful place to write. Friend thanks the staff at the Alcuin Library at the College of Saint Benedict and Saint John's University for their research support and his colleagues in the Department of Political Science for their feedback. Finally, we are grateful to our wives for their love and support during the publication process.

We gratefully acknowledge the permission of Wiley Press to draw upon our article "The Rise of Han-Centrism and What It Means for International Politics," originally published in *Studies in Ethnicity and Nationalism* 17, no. 1 (June 2017), and are grateful to editors Anastasia Voronkova and Justyna Salamonska for their aid in the submission and review process. We also thank the anonymous reviewers for their comments.

Finally, we thank Tom Swanson, our editor at Potomac Books, for his interest in this book and his assistance throughout the publication process. We also are indebted to Elaine Otto for her excellent copyediting and Ann Baker and Natalie O'Neal for navigating us through the Scylla and Charybdis of the work's progression from manuscript to book.

1 The Problem of Han-Centrism

It has been China's dream for a century to become the world's leading nation.
—Liu Mingfu, *The China Dream*, 2015

Whether China and the United States are destined to compete for domination in international politics is a major question facing both states as well as the global community. Accordingly, understanding the reasons for Chinese actions in international politics is essential. Academics and U.S. policy makers debate whether China's rise will overturn the present international order or may be accommodated and evolve within it. Critical questions revolve around what China wants, under what circumstances China will use force to advance its aims, and whether its rise will provoke a war or intense security competition with the United States, India, Japan, the Philippines, or Vietnam, or an allied coalition of these states.

There are many reasons for Chinese activities, and Beijing's actions may be usefully studied from various angles.[1] While seeking to comprehend the implications of China's rise for international relations, academics and policy makers have offered two broadly different perspectives on China's behavior.

One side perceives China as ambitious and confrontational. It argues that China will attempt to replace the liberal international order with a system that better reflects and supports its economic and political interests.[2] Referred to as the "China threat" school of thought, it suggests that heavy-handed Chinese policies in the region, notably territorial disputes in the East and South China Seas, will cause intense competition with the United States and other states in the region.

The second school adopts a more optimistic view of China's rise, pointing to China's growing involvement in multilateral institutions, dependence on international trade, and strong partnerships on pertinent global issues.[3] For this camp, China's interests are believed to be compatible with the present international order. In essence, China's rise may bring with it some political hiccups, but China is ultimately a status quo power. Consequently, the People's Republic of China (PRC) is not willing to overturn the international order that has made it increasingly wealthy.

However, because conflict and cooperation in international politics are not mutually exclusive, and because of the complexity of China's development, its study requires a more nuanced approach that pays particular attention to the ways in which domestic factors, such as historical memory, can cause conflictual or cooperative behavior. In fact, this amalgamation of behavior is captured in China's relationships with Taiwan, Japan, and the United States, which may be defined as a combination of hot economics and cold politics. Our concern is that the politics are likely to become considerably colder.

Acknowledging the importance of domestic variables, recent research has explored the influence of nationalism on Chinese foreign policy making.[4] A number of studies have identified the dimensions of Chinese nationalism, pointing out that some are more aggressive than others.[5] For example, Chinese premier Xi Jinping's call for "the great rejuvenation of the Chinese nation" or the "Chinese Dream" has been supported by a growing wave of popular nationalism among younger segments of the population, referred to by some as the "angry youth" (*fen qing* [愤青]).[6]

The xenophobia, chauvinism, and ethnocentrism associated with this nationalist movement was on full display in September 2012 during the country's annual National Humiliation Day when violent anti-Japanese protests in major Chinese cities caused many Japanese firms to shut down.[7] Such an outburst of nationalism is hardly new, as antiforeign protests appear to be a fixture of Chinese domestic and international politics.[8] But what is becoming especially worrisome is the relationship between Chinese nationalism and its aspirations. A component of the Chinese Dream is, in essence, to reestablish China's central position in Asia, not through conquest, as there is only modest evidence of this in the East and South China Seas so far, but to recover what has been lost in terms of position in global affairs and in a confidence of innate superiority. This recovery requires restoring China's status as the dominant state in international politics.

Despite the recognition of China's aggressive nationalism, the identities and narratives shaping this movement are less understood, and the study of their effects on foreign policy making is relatively underdeveloped. In particular, little attention has been paid to group identification, historical memory, and the racial discourses associated with such assertive nationalist sentiment, which can easily be found throughout the Chinese blogosphere and during protests against Japan and the United States or recalcitrant minority groups within the country like the Tibetans and Uighurs. Kevin Carrico and Peter H. Gries do well to note the absence of any serious discussion on race and racism in the study of Chinese nationalism and national identity. On this point, they write: "There are many taboos in China studies: the 'three Ts' of Tiananmen, Tibet, and Taiwan are the best known. Yet no taboo is more diligently policed than the subject of racism in Chinese nationalism," and "despite revealing studies on racism in China . . . scholarship on Chinese nationalism remains largely silent on the issue."[9]

Chinese racialized nationalism, as Carrico and Gries put it, has many perceived enemies, both domestic and foreign, and at the center of this aggressive and chauvinist form of nationalism is what we refer to as

Han-centrism, which asserts that the Han Chinese are culturally and racially superior to other groups in China and outside of it. These Han nationalists have called for a China for the Chinese, that is, Han—as the Han equate to the Chinese—and seek to advance ideas and policies that will allow the country to reclaim the prosperity stolen by foreign powers. This occurred during the "Century of Humiliation," usually delineated by the start of the First Opium War in 1839 until the Communist victory in 1949, when the country was too weak to protect itself from European, American, and Japanese colonial depredations.

As a result, this movement has been supportive of China's aggressive posture in the East and South China Seas. Equally worrisome is the fact that it supports a fundamentally new international system—a China that is committed to changing the rules, norms, and practices of the established international order to suit China. In short, this movement actively seeks to replace the United States as the dominant state in international politics.

The Central Argument

This book explores the roots of Han-centrism, implications of Chinese hypernationalism for international relations, and how the United States should respond, including working with countries in the region to mitigate its effects. Building on the work of Stephen Van Evera, we consider Han-centrism to be a form of hypernationalism with distinct social Darwinian and culturally chauvinistic dimensions.[10] That is to say, within this shared identity, the Han Chinese are considered to be racially pure and the true descendants of the "ancestral nation" (*zuguo* [祖国]). Furthermore, since the anti-Manchu revolutionaries of the late Qing dynasty, the Han way of life is portrayed as more advanced and disciplined than the "primitive" cultures of the non-Han, particularly the minority groups in the country.[11] Others have referred to this racialized understanding of ethnic groups inside and outside China as "Han racism" or the "great Han mentality."[12]

In our study, we will use Han-centrism as the equivalent of Han hypernationalism, or virulent Han nationalism. We prefer the term Han-centrism because it better captures the phenomenon we are studying—the self-referential and privileged aspect of Han identity. That is, the humiliation, shame, and foreign threat narratives are based on the experiences of the Han—emphatically not the fifty-five other ethnic groups in the country—and are considered by Han-centrists as synonymous with China.

Our argument has important implications for both Chinese domestic and international politics, especially as China's economic and military growth continues.[13] Han-centric reactions are often triggered by perceived threats to China's growth and development to reach its rightful place in foreign relations. For example, following the 2009 anti-Asian riots in Papua New Guinea, in which the local population looted Chinese-owned trade shops and bars in protest of unfair labor practices, comments on the *China News* website revealed virulent racism and nationalistic sentiment among many Chinese netizens:

> We should revive the slave system, and put all black people in chains. These black bastards eat Chinese, buy Chinese, and still want to kill Chinese. Typical slave behavior. When our nation is a bit stronger, whenever there's an incident like this, retribution will be swift, just like this year in the western regions. Chinese people work hard. So when they go abroad, they prosper, and locals are envious. What can you do? A person far from home is despised (*ren li xiang jian*), so knuckle down.[14]

Such xenophobic and chauvinistic attitudes are also directed at ethnic minorities in China. Uighurs, in particular, are all too often targets of racism. As journalist Blaine Kaltman writes, "Han-Uighur relations are colored by racist attitudes. Many told me that the Uighur are a 'fierce' and 'unreasonable' people and that they have a 'primitive mentality' and are 'apathetic to development.' . . . Their problem is that they just don't care. They don't care to be modern. They don't seem to care about anything."[15]

Like the Uighur, Africans studying and working in China, a group also perceived as socially disruptive, frequently experience overt discrimination, as "rising racism, police harassment, and an increasingly stringent and corrupt visa system dominated by Chinese middlemen has made life difficult for even the most successful." For the Africans living in major cities like Guangzhou, life is not what they expected: "Many Africans express feelings of helplessness, humiliation, and anger, railing against the harassment, racism, and indifference they face. 'Africans are treated like cockroaches here.'"[16]

Since the 1990s, the Chinese Communist Party (CCP) has promoted nationalistic rhetoric through patriotic education campaigns and propaganda, with the goal of bolstering political legitimacy and unifying the population as the country goes through profound economic and social changes.[17] In this sense, the CCP has tried to promote nationalism domestically while downplaying the "China threat" image internationally. Xi Jinping's "China Dream," and its call for "national rejuvenation," has effectively tapped into the sense of vulnerability, humiliation, and revenge at the core of Han-centrism, which in turn has enabled the CCP to rally support in opposition to foreign pressure over a variety of issues ranging from human rights violations to territorial disputes. In fact, not only have Xi's "historical allusions" been well received among the Han nationalists, but many have demanded that the Chinese government take a more aggressive stance on key regional issues.[18]

Bringing domestic factors into the study of China's foreign relations is empirically difficult given informal mechanisms and the dearth of information available on decision-making processes, such as the degree of influence the military and bureaucratic factions have on foreign policy.[19] Just as many Kremlinologists struggled to understand the effects of nationalism and communism on an obsessively secretive Soviet foreign policy apparatus during the Cold War, the lack of transparency in elite Chinese decision making has presented difficulties.

However, recent research has suggested that an autonomous nationalist public does possess a degree of influence over the CCP's political decision making.[20] In particular, our research on the revival of Han exceptionalism has found that Han-centrism appears to be promoted and reproduced at the top by the political elite and at the bottom by nationalist elements like the "angry youth" bloggers and those in the diaspora. In this sense, we consider Han-centrism to be a form of "latent nationalism" in which the Chinese elite create the means for its expression and influence on Chinese domestic and international political behavior.[21] Thus in our account, Han-centrism is most frequently an instrument to be used by these groups. At the same time, we do not want to dismiss or minimize the fact that Han-centric beliefs are truly accepted by the Han, even non-Han minorities, in China, including Chinese decision makers, intellectuals, and journalists. Han-centrism is indeed an instrument, but it is also a firmly held belief, as patriotism may be in the United States, a love of "la France" for the French, or "Mother Russia" for the Russians.

The Significance of the Study

There is no greater question in contemporary international politics than "How does China see the world?" While there are competing discourses in China on the issue of how China sees itself and its place in the world today and in the years to come, what is worrisome for the future of global stability is the outpouring of Han-centrism accompanying China's rapid growth.[22] Historically such ethnocentric sentiment is to be expected and has occurred with the upsurge of other great powers from Britain to Japan.

What is far more disturbing is the deeply rooted cultural chauvinism, ethnocentrism, and xenophobia that appear to be influencing the Chinese elite, who are in control of an emerging superpower that is likely to be, in time, the world's dominant state. In sum, the concern is that Chinese foreign policy decision making is affected by Han-centrism, making intense security competition and conflict with its neighbors and the United States more likely, if not determinative.[23] We recognize that there are many potential avenues to conflict between the United States and China: systemic causes of conflict, such as alliance pathologies, unit level causes, such as bureaucratic interests, and perhaps individual motivations as well.[24] Historically, of course, a virulent nationalism in the rising superpower is a dangerous unit level cause of conflict.[25]

Second, if China does become dominant, the rest of the world is going to have to adapt to the new values advanced by China. This means that all of the stakeholders in the present international liberal order, developed largely by Great Britain and the United States after World War II, are likely to find it more difficult to advance fundamental western concepts of free trade, individual liberty, and human rights. In many cases, the opposite of what the West values will be the new "rules of the road" in international politics. Western elites have yet to consider what will be lost if a hypernationalistic China were to become the world's dominant state, as opposed to a pragmatic China.[26]

Third, this issue is understudied. Despite the importance of China's rise, there is only a modest literature on Chinese nationalism, ethnocentrism, and racism and their impact on foreign policy.[27] There is even less on the racial component. The combination of nationalism and racial identity in Han-centrism is best addressed in Frank Dikötter's pathbreaking and sterling scholarship.[28] But beyond a small number of scholars, few address the racial elements of Han identity. Concerning the racial aspect of Han-centrism, Rotem Kowner and Walter Demel argue that "there is no justification for this oversight" on racism in East Asia by scholarly and policy communities.[29]

Our study differs from these excellent works. First, our focus is on the foreign policy consequences of Han-centrism rather than its domestic aspect. We acknowledge the importance of its domestic impact, but our scholarship will center principally on the international implications. Second, our study provides greater contextualization and analytical penetration of Han-centrism and Chinese nationalism due to the long history and considerable complexities shrouding Chinese national identity and China's foreign policies.

Counterarguments

While the literature on Chinese nationalism is, indeed, vast and cannot be covered fully here, one key takeaway is that the study of nationalism in China does not fit neatly into previous research on national identity. According to Wenfang Tang and Benjamin Darr, China was never fully colonized. Nonetheless, as the authors suggest, "While the history of each country may have unique attributes, states always have an interest in promoting national identity," which in turn requires us to study the ways in which a country constructs and promotes its national identity.[30]

A second key point is that China has not a single coherent nationalism but rather many nationalist narratives. Among these, state-led (elite) nationalism and ethnic (popular) nationalism have received a great deal of attention, and rightfully so, as they are thought to have a significant influence on modern Chinese society, particularly domestic and foreign policy making.[31]

These two forms of nationalism do not exist separately but instead interact and shape one another. In fact, since the early days of the Mao period, there has been growing tension between the state-sanctioned, multicultural nationalism of the Chinese Communist Party and the much older and divisive ethnic nationalism. For example, Nimrod Baranovitch's work on the changing representation of the non-Han in Chinese textbooks reveals that the "Han-exclusivist vision of Chinese history" remained a dominant narrative until the curriculum reforms of the 1970s and early 1980s when the more inclusive multicultural narrative was introduced, which attempted to highlight the histories and perspectives of the non-Han minority.[32] However, the experiences of ethnic minorities are still marginalized, and their portrayal in textbooks is often stereotypical and reflective of the Han nationalist narrative.[33]

These studies suggest that the dominant Han narrative, in which "Chinese" means Han, is deeply embedded in Chinese society. This poses a serious challenge to the multicultural narrative, according to Jason Patent, in that "the contrast between 'Han' and 'minority' can be easily extended to 'Chinese' and 'foreign,' and often is, whether consciously or unconsciously."[34] One example of this can be seen in Han-Tibetan and Han-Uighur relations and the tensions that often are present in their interactions.

With this emerging narrative of Han supremacy, Gray Tuttle argues that "Beijing's hard-line policies are not merely a reflection of the central state's desire to cement its authority over distant territories but also an expression of deep-seated ethnic prejudice and racism at the core of contemporary Chinese society."[35] In this sense, it appears that the CCP is playing a dangerous game as it tries to balance these two forms of nationalism to achieve political and geostrategic interests, both domestically and internationally. Ethnic nationalism serves as a "double-edged sword" in that it is an instrument to strengthen regime stability, but it comes at the cost of "heightened awareness of ethnic identity in a multiethnic state like China," which in turn can threaten national unity and political authority.[36]

For example, when confronted with territorial disputes in the East and South China Seas, calls for independence in Xinjiang, Tibet, or in cross-strait relations with Taiwan, the CCP, despite its multicultural rhetoric, often embraces the more aggressive ethnic nationalism to gain popular support and to pressure foreign governments. Ruben Gonzalez-Vicente aptly calls China's use of racial essentialism in international relations an example of "extraterritorial racial sovereignty." Addressing China relationships with countries in the region like Malaysia with large populations of ethnic Chinese, Gonzalez-Vincente argues that the government uses overseas Chinese (*huaqiao*) as bridges "to assist with the country's economic and civilizational ambitions" in that "imagined biological ties produce a distinct architecture of state power that is to some extent delinked from territory and which ultimately legitimizes intervention."[37] A similar argument has been made regarding overseas Chinese workers in Africa and accusations of neocolonial business practices that resulted in not only anti-Chinese protests but also outbursts of aggressive Han nationalist sentiment as seen in the 2009 anti-Asian riots in Papua New Guinea mentioned earlier.[38]

It is important to note that within the literature, some have insisted that the nationalism framework is a flawed perspective, one that is theoretically underdeveloped, in the context of contemporary China.[39] Others have taken this argument further by suggesting that the intensity of Chinese nationalism has been exaggerated. In the latter case, Alastair Iain Johnston argues that Chinese nationalism is, in fact, not rising but declining, especially among the younger generation.[40] While Johnston's survey study of urban Chinese takes an innovative approach that offers insight into the complexities of nationalism in China, his analysis does not include important categories of nationalism found in the literature, such as aggressive, assertive, and pragmatic.

Since China has been shown to have many nationalisms, and its own experience with nationalism and national identity differs from the study of nationalism in general, failure to account for these other dimensions limits an analysis of the degree of ethnocentrism in Chinese nationalism as well as how confident we can be that Chinese nationalism is not rising. Traditional measures on nationalism may tell us very little about nation making in contemporary China.

For example, Johnston concludes that the younger generation appears less nationalistic than the older generation because a smaller percentage of young Chinese of the patriotic education generation believe "China is a better country than most" or are willing to support the government "even when it is wrong," which he interprets as an absence of nativism and blind support commonly found in nationalist movements. However, when we consider that national humiliation, weakness, and shame are important dimensions of the patriotic education campaigns, it is not that surprising that the younger generation is more critical of the government.[41] Many of the "angry youth" see China as transitioning from "humiliation to glory," and they criticize the policies of the CCP for being soft on issues that are perceived to be obstacles to China's return to its rightful position of power in Asia.[42] Furthermore, on social media platforms like Weibo, the angry youth have attacked the Chinese government for "its failure to protect its citizens during moments of overseas crisis," such as "the horror endured by the ethnic Chinese community during the 1998 anti-Chinese riots in Indonesia."[43]

As the work of William Callahan shows, the national humiliation embedded within Chinese public culture "is not deployed just in a predictably xenophobic way but also in a self-critical examination of Chineseness."[44] A sense of shame defines Chinese national consciousness because the humiliation experienced is not solely a result of foreign exploitation but also domestic corruption committed by the ruling class. Moreover, this self-critical examination of Chineseness is not new but historically rooted in Han identity and can be seen in the rhetoric of anti-Manchu nationalists during the late Qing dynasty. During this time, according to Dikötter, many Han revolutionaries believed that the nation had failed: "'We Chinese are less than black slaves' was a common expression. Humiliation fostered outrage and created a sense of resentment that was favourable to the nationalist message."[45]

In fact, the contemporary popular nationalist movement in China has been one of the CCP's toughest critics, often pushing the government to be more aggressive on domestic issues and diplomatic disputes, particularly western meddling, believed to be impediments to China's rejuvenation.[46] For example, during the 2012–13 anti-Japanese protest in mainland China over the Diaoyu (Senkaku) Islands, many nationalists criticized the CCP's weakness on the issue and pressured the government to respond more forcefully.[47] While many young Chinese may well be unsatisfied with the government and unwilling to support its actions blindly, they continue to display a fair amount of hypernationalism.

With this in mind, the study of Chinese nationalism should go beyond debating whether or not nationalism is rising, Instead, we should recognize that the Chinese are more nationalistic in some ways than in others. In particular, the Chinese appear to be more nationalistic in their reactions to foreign condemnations of China, their greater pride in China's achievements, and the way they approach international affairs.[48] While the level and intensity of nationalism in China is not easily measured, there are a number of studies that analyze patriotic displays and antiforeigner protests in China and conclude that nationalism has been, and continues to be, an important component of Chinese identity and thus a variable in the study of regime legitimacy, foreign policy, and how China sees its place in the world.[49]

Furthermore, as Jackson Woods and Bruce Dickson suggest, an analysis of the causes of nationalism in China requires a fair amount of nuance in that "those who wave flags to show their patriotic pride are not necessarily the same ones who wield hammers to bash foreign cars."[50] Building from these perspectives, we argue that Han-centrism is a particularly influential form of hypernationalism in China that has been facilitated, and at times emboldened, by the CCP's continued emphasis on humiliation, foreign exploitation, and Han supremacy.

Outline of the Chapters

Chapter 2 discusses Han-centrism and identifies its roots. Through an analysis of the political writings of Han nationalists during the late Qing dynasty and the 1911 Xinhai Revolution, such as that of Sun Yat-sen, Zhang Binglin, Zou Rong, and Liang Qichao, we examine the racial thinking and traumatized memory that led to Han-centrism. These late Qing radicals played an influential role in the development of an ethnic Han identity and an "ancestral nation" that served as the foundation for a "racial revolution" (*zhongzu geming* [种族革命]).[51]

Chapter 3 places Han-centrism in a contemporary and cultural context. Chinese nationalism contains many facets and can be fragmented and is thus similar to nationalist beliefs held by many peoples and states in history. What we identify is that Chinese nationalism has evolved from greater emphasis on the ideological foundation of Maoism to an ethnic one, based on Han identity. Second, we submit that Han supremacy shapes modern Chinese society and foreign policy.

Chapter 4 explores why this particular strain of Chinese nationalism is worrisome for the stability of international politics given the increasing power of China and its concomitant growing ability to shape norms and values. The study of Han-centrism in foreign policy provides us with insight into how Beijing's worldview will shape the future of China and of international politics. The racial identity and collective memory associated with Han-centrism is a cohesive force that the Chinese political elite can exploit. Here racial beliefs often feed hypernationalism, and as China continues to expand its sphere of influence regionally and internationally, it needs the unwavering patriotic support of its population at home and abroad. Han-centrism makes this possible by supporting and legitimating an "us versus them" mentality that fuels security competition and mistrust between China and other nations.

Chapter 5 considers the five major asymmetries for U.S. leaders that result from the Han-centric worldview and that will become increasingly important in the "war of ideas" that has already started between Beijing and Washington. In a competition with the People's Republic of China, the United States must explore all of its advantages and all of the weaknesses of China that may provide an asymmetry for the United States. This study examines one such asymmetry, the strategic consequences of Chinese Han-centrism.

The first asymmetry is that Han-centrism provides empirical evidence of how Beijing will treat other countries if China becomes dominant. One of the key insights into Chinese future behavior is its behavior in the past when it was the hegemon of Asia. For the Han nationalists, China is the center of the universe, and all others are inferior to varying degrees. This makes it more challenging to find allies.

The second is that China's Han-centrism allows the United States to undermine China in the Global South. The essence of the Chinese message to these states is a straightforward rhetorical query: have Americans or Europeans ever treated you as equals? In contrast, China portrays itself as an apolitical rising superpower that does business in your country, pays a fair price for your commodities, and builds your infrastructure with no strings attached. The United States can counter the expansion of Chinese influence by tying into the messages stated above but also adding the point that there is no culture of antiracism in China, and so there is little hope for change.

The third is that it permits a positive image of the United States to be advanced in contrast to China. The stark fact is, when compared with a hypernationalistic China, it is easy to convey to the rest of the world the message that the United States is open and inclusive, whereas China is not. This is because such openness is in accord with the principles of the United States and its history and especially so since the civil rights movement of the 1960s.

The fourth for the United States is that calling attention to Han-centrism allows political and ideological alliances with the United States to be strengthened. Political alliances particularly with the developing world are an obvious benefit. Equally important are the ideological alliances that the United States may augment. Intellectual circles in Europe, Canada, and the United States value multiracial and multicultural societies. Journalists and media opinion makers frequently share a multiracial and multicultural vision of their societies as well. Yet they have not treated the problem of Han-centrism with the attention it deserves.

The fifth is that United States leaders must recognize that Han-centrism is a cohesive force for the Chinese government. The country is a civilization, and this brings them great strength. While it does benefit the CCP, it also gives the United States an advantage. The lack of any desire by the Chinese government to self-reflect on the outgrowth of hypernationalism means that there is little to no motivation to address it. Accordingly, a powerful message may be that China will not change because it has no desire to do so. In essence, with China, "What you see is what you get, and you had better get used to it because it's not going to change."

The last chapter offers the study's fundamental conclusions: Han-centrism is a complex phenomenon. It contains many risks for the Chinese government and people, but it also provides advantages. For the United States, it is a major asymmetry that it may exploit with major countries, regions like Africa, as well as with important opinion makers in international politics. But beyond the United States, for all actors in the global community, Han-centrism provides empirical evidence of how Beijing will treat other international actors as China becomes increasingly more powerful. An analysis of Han-centrism in contemporary Chinese society makes clear why those who have a vested interest in the present order, especially advocates of racial equality and human rights, need to consider the implications of the rise of a hypernationalistic China for their political ideals.

2 The Origins of Han-Centrism

> There has been a great task on which, during the last five thousand years,
> our ancestors have continually expended much effort. . . . What is this
> task? To give it a name I call it "the expansion of the Chinese race."
> —Liang Qichao, "Review of China's Progress," 1922

Nationalism, as Anthony Smith suggests, is a product of deep historical roots in culture and shared history but also, as famously noted by Benedict Anderson, an "imagined community" constructed by the political elite through the manipulation of cultural and ethnic symbols.[1] Through the embrace of modernity, notably western science and technology, the elite seek to create and maintain a particular national identity that serves as the symbol of the nation and means to obtain legitimacy and rally support. As Stuart Hall succinctly puts it, "National cultures help to 'stitch up' differences" into a coherent identity.[2] This process of homogenization, however, is "arduously constructed" and often involves violence, segregation, censorship, and various forms of political and economic coercion.[3]

Our objective is to place Han-centrism within the broader literature on nationalism, a useful theoretical framework that some have argued is absent in many studies on Chinese nationalism.[4] Therefore, by synthesizing the culturalists' and constructivists' perspectives, we argue that Han-centrism is not only "ethnosymbolic," that is, a shared set of belief systems, cultural values, and memories, but also a product of elite manipulation of these cultural symbols, which have certainly evolved over time. In the context of Chinese nationalism and national identity, such an approach is valuable since, as James Leibold correctly notes, "The fluidity of nationalist thought in China defies rigid distinctions between tradition and modernity. . . . Modernization in China was not a linear and teleological process but rather a complex and relational dialogue between past, present, and future."[5]

Furthermore, with the inclusion of international relations theories, particularly work on the causes of ethnonational violence, we can better comprehend the ways in which race is deeply intertwined with nationalism. Previous work in the field of international relations has revealed the dynamic factors that influence national identity formation, factors that played a significant role in shaping Han identity and nationalism during the late Qing dynasty (1644–1912) and the 1911 Xinhai Revolution, which led to the eventual overthrow of the Manchu regime. Most important, this Han-centrism continues to influence Chinese nationalism today. Moreover, through an analysis of the ways in which late Qing intellectuals constructed and articulated the cultural and racial symbols of Han identity, we can gain a better appreciation of how identity, history, and nation come together to justify violence in the establishment of nationhood and sovereignty, as well as a deeper understanding of how Han-centrism serves as an enduring dimension of Chinese nationalism.

Han-Centrism as a Form of Hypernationalism

For the study of Han-centrism, earlier work on hypernationalism and ethnonational violence in the field of international relations is a useful place to start, as this line of research provides a great deal of insight into the nation-making process and why certain forms of nationalism become violent and aggressive while others do not. Work by Stephen Van Evera, in particular, offers a detailed breakdown of the remote and proximate causes of nationalistic violence. For the former, Van Evera lists political status, relationship with national diaspora, perception of other nationalities, and respect for national minority populations as leading proximate causes. Regarding remote causes, he identifies three specific conditions: structural factors, such as geography (e.g., defensibility and international recognition of boundaries) and demography (e.g., the presence or absence of intermingling populations); political/environmental factors, such as the resolution or continuation of past crimes (e.g., the oppression of one group by another); and perceptional factors, such as nationalist self-image and image of outsiders.[6]

Furthermore, Van Evera argues that some types of nationalism are more aggressive than others, with the most dangerous nationalist regimes being those that require some degree of popular support and are governed by unrepresentative elites. Within this type of regime, hypernationalism, that is, the belief that one's nation is superior and, therefore, has the legitimacy to dominate inferior nations, and militarism, or the belief that war is noble and beneficial to society, play defining roles in that the political elite and policy makers stir up these xenophobic and negative emotions to unify the population during periods of social, political, and/or economic change.[7]

Similar research has noted that at the core of hypernationalism are nationalist myths and reminders of victimization that can produce fear and mass hostility.[8] As Jacques Bertrand submits, group fears and grievances are deeply embedded in the context in which ethnic identities are constructed and mobilized.[9] While eliciting ethnic chauvinism to promote hostile emotions toward out-groups is often used by regimes attempting to solidify power, Stuart Kaufman warns that such a strategy can backfire. In other words, chauvinist emotions can be channeled to gain or maintain power, but can also easily create a "symbolic politics trap" in which the political elite "may be unable to calm those emotions later, even if they wish to reverse course and moderate their policies."[10]

Furthermore, as the chauvinist emotions become more intense, leaders that do not adopt extreme positions can lose legitimacy, in turn causing the regime to replace them. Thus the extreme policies of mass hostility can lead to a spiral of increasing ethnonational violence.[11]

These perspectives suggest that cultural values and collective memory play important roles within the mass hostility of ethnic violence. For example, Jonathan Spencer's study of ethnic conflict in the Sinhala areas of Sri Lanka found "cultural patterning in the actual manner of collective violence," such that a combination of organized political violence by the elite, the collective memory of Sinhala-Tamil conflict and resistance, and the spread of rumor and fear of the Other led to aggressive behavior.[12] Historical memory is an important variable here because the "psychological consequences of intergroup violence can linger among members of previously victimized groups for generations after peace is restored."[13] Essentially, trauma is passed down to the next generation and can be just as humiliating and infuriating to the younger generations. This is especially true when the elite constantly remind the next generation, usually in the form of education programs, of past humiliation and exploitation committed by foreign powers. Research on war memory and commemoration captures this psychological process well.[14]

Furthermore, many have pointed out the central roles that race and ethnicity play in historical memory, as the formation of an ethnic community requires widely shared memories.[15] Ethnic identity, in this view, is understood to be historically constructed, an ongoing process that requires the manipulation of "historical truths" and "contemporary facts," which often seeks to draw clear boundaries between the in-group and the out-group.[16] According to Donald Horowitz, this manipulation is often done by the elite, as ethnicity "embodies an element of emotional intensity that can be readily aroused when the group's interests are thought to be at stake."[17] In this sense, ethnicity works "in and through categories, schemas, common-sense knowledge, symbols, elite and vernacular discourse, institutional norms, organizational routines, public ceremonies, and private interactions."[18]

Along similar lines, David Jack Eller argues that the ethnic group defines "'what we really are' in terms of 'what we were.'" That is to say, members of an ethnic group often look to the past, which usually entails a fair amount of "misremembering," to construct an "authentic" ethnic identity with deep historical roots. Through this understanding, Eller suggests that "cultural past and tradition" legitimize ethnic identity in that ethnic groups are "pursuing an interest using culture or history as their claim and their weapon."[19] Like Eller, Akbar Ahmed notes that ethnic groups use past grievances as a source of animosity and justification for ethnopolitical violence, with honor, glory, and mythology serving as key components of aggressive ethnic nationalism.[20] This racial/ethnic animosity can contribute to outbursts of ethnic conflict as well as facilitate intolerance toward out-group members.[21] Here racism presents itself in the form of what Peter Wade refers to as "super nationalism," such that notions of national heritage and culture are reconfigured into "more powerful and virulent ideas of national inheritance, the national body, national purity, and aesthetic ideals of national men (and women)."[22]

Turning to the case of Han-centrism, perceptions of other ethnic groups and nationalities (which should be considered a proximate cause), along with political and perceptional factors such as unresolved past crimes and nationalist self-image (which should be conceived of as remote causes), have produced a deeply rooted and pervasive form of hypernationalism that can be traced back to the anti-Manchu intellectuals of the late Qing dynasty. While some work has already addressed the defining features of Chinese collective memory, little to no attention has been given to how shared memory and trauma, often evoked by the elite for political gain, produce a Han-centric hypernationalism.

A group's fears, grievances, and cultural interpretations serve as the context in which ethnonational identities are constructed and mobilized.

According to Maurice Halbwach, memories of the past, including those of trauma and glory, are social constructions shaped by present concerns, such that "the beliefs, interests, and aspirations of the present shape the various views of the past as they are manifested respectively in every historical epoch."[23] With this in mind, the following sections address the historical roots of Han-centrism, with special attention given to the narratives that make up Han-centric historical memory.

Trauma, Humiliation, and the Other in the Han-Centric Worldview

A fair amount of research has already begun to explore the trauma underlying Chinese nationalism. Most notably, work by Zheng Wang, William Callahan, and Peter Gries highlights the influence that the "Century of Humiliation" (1839–1949) has on Chinese national identity and collective memory.[24] During this period, China lost its great power status, specifically its hegemonic position in Asia, to exploitative foreign powers, starting with British and French intervention during the first Opium War, followed by continued western and Japanese imperialism, and ending with Mao Zedong's establishment of the People's Republic of China in 1949. During this time, China was forced to comply with humiliating "unequal treaties" that required the Chinese to cede territory, open ports, pay indemnities, and make numerous concessions to foreign influences. In fact, as Wang notes, "foreign invasions and lost wars" serve as the core of Han Chinese chosen trauma, in which foreign "devils" (*guizi*) interfered in the domestic affairs of the country, such as arming and siding with certain warlords, and essentially reduced China to a "semicolonial society."[25]

Moreover, China's cultural achievements and status as the Middle Kingdom were challenged and the Sinocentric worldview of *tianxia* (the realm under heaven) was forcibly overturned by a Eurocentric worldview that portrayed China as the inferior "sick man" of Asia.[26] Recognizing the collapse of the status quo ushered in by foreign invasion, late Qing intellectual Liang Qichao wrote, "I read Western newspapers and they report on . . . the disorder in the Chinese polity. . . . This has been going on for the past few decades." Since October 1896 "they have even more openly and brazenly publicized how wild and uncivilized the Chinese are, how ignorant and dishonest, how empty Chinese Confucianism is. The meaning is clear: they will eliminate China at once."[27]

Most upsetting for late Qing intellectuals like Liang was China's inability to culturally assimilate the invaders, as was often the case in the past. Rather, as many Chinese intellectuals at the time saw it, the invaders were trying to assimilate China. Thus, within the narrative of humiliation, foreign powers deny China its status as "the center of the world" and the "only true civilization," and as a result, according to Zheng Wang, "the Chinese lost a bit of their national myth of greatness."[28]

However, to understand how the humiliation narrative continues to shape hypernationalism in China today, it is necessary to examine the origins of this Han-centrism, as less attention has been given to the ways in which the Han (anti-Manchu) nationalists during the late Qing dynasty and the 1911 Xinhai Revolution articulated narratives of race and nation, and most notably a Han-centered collective memory, within the contexts of revolution, resistance, and possible extermination at the hands of encroaching foreign spheres of influence. Henrietta Harrison argues that the arrival of western forces played a role in the transition from culturalism to nationalism, as many of the late Qing intellectuals (both Han reformists and revolutionaries), notably Yan Fu ([严复] 1854–1921), Zhang Binglin ([章炳麟] 1868–1936), Liang Qichao ([梁启超] 1873–1929), Zou Rong ([邹容] 1885–1905), and Sun Yat-sen ([孙中山] 1866–1925), called for an increase of national consciousness and China's modernization through the pursuit of wealth and power.[29] In this sense, the Han intellectuals embraced western concepts and ideologies, notably western understandings of "race" found within the racial sciences of the late nineteenth century, to transform China into a racially homogeneous nation-state that could compete with modernized foreign powers, especially those from the West.[30]

During the late Qing regime and the Xinhai Revolution, opposition to Manchu rule served as the intellectual background of the ethnocentric and nationalist ideology of many nineteenth-century Chinese thinkers.[31] The work of Edward Rhoads on Han-Manchu relations highlights the process in which Han intellectuals criticized the Qing court and forged a separate identity. First, these revolutionaries argued that the Manchu were an alien, barbarian group that emerged from the periphery of China's civilized core. That is, the Manchu were not considered to be "Chinese," an identity that solely belonged to the Han. Second, they committed horrendous crimes against the Han, which included both unthinkable violence and the forced acceptance of barbaric customs and practices, such as changes in dress and hairstyle. These grievances only intensified through occupation, discrimination, and segregation of the Han by the Qing regime.[32]

Within the newly emerging Han-centric worldview, the Manchu became the enemy, a symbol of threat and otherness. More important, through the articulation of the Manchu as the ethnic and cultural Other, Han radicals were able to construct the racial and cultural symbols of Han nationalism, as well as define the "ancestral nation" (zuguo [祖国]) that would later serve as the foundation for a "racial revolution" (zhongzu geming [种族革命]).[33] In other words, by defining the Manchu as alien, these intellectuals insisted that China was under illegitimate foreign occupation, and as a result they had the right to defend their ancestral homeland and reassert their rightful place in Asia.

Although some Han intellectuals pushed for a universal nationalism, one that would include the Manchu as well as the other ethnic groups, revolutionaries like Zhang Binglin rejected the universality and pushed for an anti-Manchu nationalist movement that would be carried out for the Han by the Han. In fact, according to Young-tsu Wong, Zhang Binglin was one of the first to articulate an anti-Manchu ideology that not only criticized the Manchu for their incompetent rule and brutality against the Han but also drew distinct racial lines between the two groups by emphasizing that "culture has its ethnic origin." Essentially, these revolutionaries believed that the Han and Manchu were incompatible, as the Manchu would refuse to assimilate to the culturally superior Han way and would instead destroy it. Therefore, "Zhang showed contempt for the Manchu race and government alike, comparing them to other inferior, barbaric, and unworthy races who had populated Chinese frontiers throughout history."[34]

Along similar lines, in *The Revolutionary Army* (1903), Zou Rong argued that the foreign Manchu are an "inferior race of nomads with wolfish ambitions." Despite their widespread adoption of Han administrative practices during the Qing dynasty, the Manchu signified backwardness, stasis, and weakness.[35] Their incompetence, corruption, and oppressive practices would only impede China's revival and recovery from foreign exploitation. As far as the revolutionaries were concerned, the Qing regime was incapable of defending China against imperialistic foreign occupiers and must be removed from power.[36]

Peter Zarrow submits that the "ugliness of the anti-Manchuism" has been overlooked, as well as the ways in which historical trauma shaped the Han nationalist narrative during the late Qing and the revolution. Within the collective memory of the late Qing radicals, the Han Chinese "had suffered deep wounds and ongoing injury" during the Manchu conquest. In particular, the violence carried out by the Manchu armies against the Han, events well captured in Wang Xiuchu's *Account of Ten Days at Yangzhou* and the similar *Account of the Jiading Massacre*, left young Han radicals "'traumatized' by foreign invasion and cultural threats." As a result, they demanded "racial revenge."[37]

These events would later serve as propaganda for the revolutionaries to gain support and challenge the Qing regime. What made such propaganda popular, according to Zarrow, was the searing "emotional condemnation" of the Manchu and the open call for racial unity; these references to humiliation and conquest were simply "designed to arouse popular anger" and enlist traumatic memory in support of their revolutionary movement.[38]

For example, in *The Revolutionary Army*, Zou Rong makes an effort to highlight the trauma experienced by the Han: "When I read the *Account of Ten Days at Yangzhou* and *Account of the Jiading Massacre*, I began weeping before I finished reading them. . . . For these two incidents, which are known to everyone, there are a hundred thousand other Yangzhous and Jiadings." Zou continues, "When I recall them, I am in anguish. . . . When those Manchu scoundrels entered China, were not those butchered by them the great-great-grandfathers of your great-great-grandfathers?" and "Were not those raped by the Manchu scoundrels the wives, daughters, or sisters of the great-great-grandfathers of your great-great-grandfathers?"[39] Similar sentiment and trauma were captured by Sun Yat-sen when he requested that an audience of Han close their eyes and "recall the history of our ancestors' blood flowing in rivers and their corpses lying everywhere."[40]

Zou and Sun's retelling of these events attempts to tap into memories of grievances, evoking what Bojana Blagojevic refers to as "ethnic emotions" of fear, hate, resentment, and rage. It also seeks to instill Han solidarity in opposition to the Manchu by drawing a connection, along with familial ties, between the past and the present.[41] According to David Pillemer, these Qing radicals "worked hard to implant violent and disturbing images implicating the Manchu" by encouraging "their audience to 'own' the traumatic experiences inflicted upon others."[42]

Using "Race" to Construct the Chinese (Han) Nation

Previous work has explored the ways in which race is understood and institutionalized within the nation-making process. Much of this research approaches race, ethnicity, and nationalism as a "single integrated domain" and notes "the extensive overlapping and blurring between race and ethnicity." This move toward a more dynamic and processual understanding of nation, ethnicity, and race, according to Rogers Brubaker, helps us better understand how ethnicity emerges "through categorical we-they distinctions drawn by actors themselves and through channeling of interaction through sets of prescriptions and proscriptions about who can interact with whom in what sorts of social relationships."[43]

Late Qing intellectuals recognized the emotional intensity rooted in ethnic identity and sought to use appeals of "us versus them" to mobilize the Han against the Manchu regime. By repositioning the Manchu as the "backward periphery," a group distinctly different from the Han, revolutionaries were able to conflate China (Zhongguo) with the Han people (Hanzu) and construct a new Han identity with a racially and culturally homogenized connection to the ancient yellow race.[44] As Prasenjit Duara notes, the nation requires a historical configuration designed to include certain groups and to exclude or marginalize others.[45] In this view, nation making requires establishing a national subject with clear boundaries of who belongs and who does not, with the out-group often viewed as a threat to the security and stability of the in-group.

For Han intellectuals at this time, the western concept of "race" and newly encountered scientific racism served as a way to draw these boundaries and construct a national (Han) subject. As a result, race would serve as "the catalyst of [Chinese] group homogeneity; it created clear boundaries by binding the in-group and distancing the out-group."[46] On this point Frank Dikötter argues that the western race–based classificatory system was easily incorporated into the intellectual landscape of nineteenth-century China, as many Chinese elite already held longstanding discriminatory views of "faraway barbarians" based on skin tone and customary practices. Here Dikötter suggests that Han intellectuals drew from "indigenous meaning," not just newly adopted western concepts, when rearticulating their Han-centric worldview.[47]

Furthermore, according to Dikötter, "The revolutionaries viewed the Han not only as a culturally distinct people with their own language and shared history, but also as a pure 'race.'"[48] Han-centrism can be seen as a useful discursive tool for crafting a national identity, as race serves as a way to erase, deny, and homogenize competing narratives and identities that threaten the nation-state. In this sense, Balibar and Wallerstein are correct to note that "racism is not an 'expression' of nationalism, but a supplement of nationalism or more precisely a supplement internal to nationalism, always in excess of it, but always indispensable to its constitution."[49]

For the anti-Manchu revolutionaries, the concept of race (*minzu*) made possible a national community composed solely of the Han race.[50] Such an identity was important to the revolutionaries, as it allowed them to justify violence against the Manchu, the historic outsider needed to define the nation, and to articulate a mono-Hanzu Chinese nation that culturally and ethnically belonged to the Han. In many ways, these revolutionaries were attempting to directly challenge the "multiethnic China" narrative that the Qing court used to equate Qing with China, win over the Han literati, and justify Manchu rule over the Han and other ethnic groups.[51] Thus, despite the efforts of the Manchu to address the "ethnic problem" through the establishment of social engineering projects, or what Mark Elliott refers to as "Qing universalism," the Han intellectuals argued that the Han were a distinct group that was superior to the "barbarians" from the periphery.[52] As Zarrow suggests, "Anti-Manchuism was more than a passing prejudice or mere revolutionary rhetoric. . . . Although it disappeared quickly after the 1911 Revolution finally erupted, it was integral to the revolutionary movement and so the founding of the Republic. To the extent revolutions are about purification, anti-Manchuism promised to expunge pollution from the body politic."[53]

Therefore, for revolutionaries like Zou Rong, the Han would lead the racial revolution (*minzu geming* [民族革命]) against the alien Manchu and thus restore China's distinct Han-ness by seeking revenge for past Han subjugation and humiliation.[54] In *The Revolutionary Army*, Zou argues that it is the responsibility of the Han to "sweep away millennia of despotism in all its forms, throw off millennia of slavishness, annihilate the five million and more of the furry and horned Manchu race," and "cleanse ourselves of 260 years of harsh and unremitting pain, so that the soil of the Chinese subcontinent is made immaculate, and the descendants of the Yellow Emperor will all become Washingtons."[55]

Zou Rong was not the only Han intellectual to advocate Han supremacy and the expansion of the Chinese race. Liang Qichao, also taking the "race as destiny" argument, wrote of the great Han revival under way: "There has been a great task on which, during the last five thousand years, our ancestors have continually expended much effort and which has never been interrupted. During the last fifty years, it still has been vigorously carried on, and furthermore, it has been fruitful." He continues, "What is this task? I call it 'the expansion of the Chinese race.' Originally our Chinese race consisted merely of a few bases in Shantung, Honan, and other places," but "during the several thousand years that followed it has been slowly growing . . . until it has become a high and peerless race, and has established this vast and majestic nation." Liang asserts, "The Chinese race has grown in two ways: through assimilation of the numerous alien tribes in and outside our territory, and through colonization by our own people on the frontiers year by year, thus enlarging our territory."[56]

Racial Revenge and the Incorporation of Social Darwinism

According to Kai-wing Chow, Chinese students studying in Japan were introduced to social Darwinism and its discourse of racist evolutionism, which they later combined with traditional understandings of race to support the creation of a Han national identity that would fit within the newly encountered and eagerly embraced "survival of the fittest" paradigm.[57] Liang is believed to be one of the first to introduce western racial sciences to the anti-Manchu rebellion and apply the social Darwinian paradigm to the Han struggle against the Manchu.[58] For the anti-Manchu intellectuals like Liang, "the yellow race was dominated by the Han people," and Han cultural traditions were responsible for advanced civilization in Asia.[59]

As the work of Timothy Cheek shows, it was during this time that the western concept of race, with its emphasis on a hierarchy of civilized and uncivilized, "began to make sense," as it supported their anti-Manchuism narrative of Han supremacy.[60] Moreover, western race theories, notably eugenics, were viewed by many as a way to simultaneously improve the Han race and counter racial stigmatism. On this point, Yuehtsen Chung argues that eugenics, race theory, and social Darwinism also served as "counterimperial discourses" that "were deployed both to resist external imperial impositions and within internal, cultural, and political disputes."[61]

With the adoption of social Darwinian thinking by both reformers and revolutionaries, "historical conceptions of inferior races" were soon translated into "a conception of a new global order of hierarchy of races and nations." As Duara notes, these Han intellectuals sought to racially purify China, as race was considered to be the "principal source of the values that it took to be fit and civilized."[62] Thus within this racial belief system of the late Qing intellectuals, race becomes the symbol of common blood and cohesion, serving as the basis of national loyalty.[63]

Furthermore, the ideas of evolution and racial struggle adopted by Han intellectuals fit well within the larger political context of western encroachment and their growing concern about conflict with more advanced civilizations that had not only military superiority but also greater amounts of political and economic power.[64] As a result, many embraced the Lamarckian paradigm, which posited that evolution occurred on a linear path with degeneration and progress on opposite ends.[65] Through the adoption of this perspective, many Han intellectuals argued that the world's population consisted of five large racial groups—yellow, white, black, brown, and red—with the Chinese race, which included the Han, falling under the yellow racial group. While the Koreans, Japanese, Tibetans, and Vietnamese were classified as subgroups of the Han, the Manchu were seen as a subgroup of the Tungus that belonged to the Siberian race.[66] Moreover, following Lamarckian thought, these racial groups were further classified as either superior or inferior, modern or primitive, with the yellow and white races more advanced and civilized and the brown, black, and red much less so.[67]

As the works of Martin Jacques and Jia Qingguo show, foreigners, traditionally described as "devils" in Chinese history, are distinguished by their skin color, with Caucasians referred to as "white devils" (*baigui* [白鬼]) and those of darker skin as "black devils" (*heigui* [黑鬼]). However, "devils" were not all regarded in the same way; white devils were perceived as "rulers" and black devils as "slaves."[68] Within this racial hierarchy, as many of the late Qing intellectuals understood it, the struggle for supremacy would inevitably occur between the yellow and white races, as the brown, black, and red races were believed to be too weak, stupid, and fragmented to pose a serious threat. Rather, many believed that the white race would eventually try to dominate the entire yellow race. Therefore, the greatest threat for the Han Chinese would eventually come from the West.

This understanding of the racial struggle is captured well by Zou: "The yellow and white races which are to be found on the globe have been endowed by nature with intelligence and fighting capacity. They are fundamentally incapable of giving way to each other." He continues: "Hence, glowering and poised for a fight, they have engaged in battle in the world of evolution, the great arena where strength and intelligence have clashed since earliest times, the great theater where for so long natural selection and progress have been played out."[69]

New fears of degeneration were exacerbated by the collective memory of trauma and humiliation shared by these late Qing intellectuals. That is, feelings of humiliation and shame caused by China's fall to foreign powers (the loss of the Middle Kingdom) now included fears of racial extinction. In order to preserve the Han race, revolutionaries believed a cohesive group was needed, made possible through racial nationalism. For these revolutionaries, success within the Darwinian struggle for survival would only come from a unifying national culture (*minzu wenhua* [民族文化]) and racial unity based on common bloodline, language, and customs, as they firmly believed that "human history was the story of 'minzu competition' (*minzu jingzheng* [民族竞争]), with different social groups struggling for evolutionary survival."[70]

This racial identity (*minzuzhuyi* [民族主义]) at the center of Han nationalism, according to Peter Harris, can be understood as "the process whereby a group or community that shares a common history, culture, language, and territory is persuaded to assert its identity in such a way that it acquires the authority to be in charge of its own affairs, usually through the creation of an independent state."[71] Many Han nationalists believed that failure to establish a strong, homogeneous Han nation would result in their extinction, much like the "barbarian red and savage black races."[72] For example, Liang declared that "India's failure to rise" was due "to limitations of the race." Following the logic of social Darwinian thinking, he believed that "all black, red, and brown peoples are in the micro-organisms of their blood and the slope of their brains quite inferior to white men. Only the yellows and the whites are not far removed from one another. Hence anything whites can do, yellows can do also."[73]

Along similar lines, Qu Qiubai ([瞿秋白] 1899–1935) wrote of the distinctions between the Hanzu and the "alien races" (*yizu* [异族]) and the need to compete with foreign powers, especially the West. On this point Qu argued: "In the historical past, the Hanzu of China was the most culturally advanced nation. . . . Nowadays, we must recognize that China's own cultural level on the world political-economic stage is rather backward. Japan is one century ahead of China. . . . Other Far Eastern *minzu* have naturally come under the influence of advanced Europe and America and are no longer under China's dominance."[74] Similarly, Yan Fu drew from the yellow-white-brown-black race categories to articulate concepts of "struggle" and "natural selection" that explained China's changing political landscape. In particular, Yan Fu contrasted western wealth and power with China's weakness, poverty, and backwardness and warned of the approaching racial struggle with the West.[75] In his view, the accumulation of power was paramount for the preservation of the Han race: "Races compete with races, and form groups and states, so that these groups and states can compete with each other. The weak will be eaten by the strong, the stupid will be enslaved by the clever," and it is "the struggle for existence which leads to natural selection and the survival of the fittest—and hence, with the human realm, to the greatest realization of human capacities."[76]

This fear of racial extermination among Han intellectuals gave way to a siege mentality in which foreign invaders would divide the country and enslave the population if the Han remained fragmented and without a strong national consciousness. To prevent the Han from becoming "slaves of an exterminated nation," Zou called on the Han to abandon their slavish behavior and transform themselves into citizens (*guomin* [国民]), as failure to do so would leave China vulnerable to cutthroat global competition, with the Han reduced to slaves ruled by numerous masters.[77]

Like Zou, Sun Yat-sen believed that preserving the ancient and superior Han race required driving out the Tartars and restoring China: "The government of China should be in the hands of the [Han] Chinese."[78] His call for "saving the nation" is further articulated in his most substantial work, the *Three People's Principles* [*Sanminzhuyi*] published in 1927. The humiliation of foreign abuse, starting with the First Opium War and continuing with Manchu rule, plays a significant role in Sun's call for the revival of Han nationalism and the reestablishment of the powerful and revered Central Kingdom: "Our old national spirit is asleep. We must awaken it. Then, our nationalism will begin to revive. When our nationalism is revived, we can go a step further and study how to restore our national standing."[79]

According to Sun, promoting nationalism would ensure the survival of the Han race, which he and the other revolutionaries believed to be the true descendants of China. On this point, he writes: "The Chinese race totals four hundred million people; of mingled races, there are only a few million Mongolians, a million or so Manchus, a few million Tibetans, and over a million Mohammedan Turks. These alien races do not number altogether more than ten million, so that, for the most part, the Chinese people are of the Han or Chinese race with common blood, common language, common religion, and common customs—a single, pure race."[80]

Sun Yat-sen's hypernationalist views are also expressed in his earlier *Manifesto of the T'ung-meng-Hui* (1905), where he writes: "Now the National Army has established the Military Government, which aims to cleanse away two hundred and sixty years of barbarous filth, restore our four-hundred-year-old fatherland, and plan for the welfare of the four hundred million people." He adds: "We recall that, since the beginning of our nation the Chinese have always ruled China, although at times alien peoples have usurped the rule. . . . Now the men of Han [i.e., the Chinese] have raised a righteous [or patriotic] army to exterminate the northern barbarians."[81]

While revolutionaries like Sun Yat-sen acknowledged Han weakness and past failures, these revolutionaries also embraced a sense of racial pride and cultural superiority.[82] The Han, according to the revolutionaries, were descendants and developers of a great civilization that originated in the Yellow River valley. Within this perspective, the Yellow Emperor (Yanhuang Zisun [炎黄子孙]), believed to be born in 2704 BC, would become a symbol of Han identity, as he was said to be the "founder of the nation politically, culturally, and biologically," with all Han Chinese seen as his children.[83] This myth of common ancestry, and the racialized thinking surrounding it, bolstered a "Great Han chauvinism" (*da hanzu zhuyi* [大汉族主义]) that supported the Han nationalist claim to China.[84]

As Orville Schell and John Delury suggest, Sun Yat-sen's call for nationalism is framed in strong social Darwinian terms such that a well-defined Han national identity is necessary for preventing racial extinction and the triumph of the white race over the yellow race. In other words, "The idea of 'China' had as much to do with protecting the Chinese people as a race and culture as it did with preserving the sovereign territory of the country."[85] However, Han revolutionaries considered states with multiple races to be inferior and prone to failure, while a nation that was "internally egalitarian and free from disputes" could "forge ahead in the evolutionary struggle of life and death." Therefore, as Duara argues, "both the global discourse of social Darwinism and the anti-Manchu politics of the Republic revolution forced a conception of the national community that was made up exclusively of the Han race."[86] While this interpretation of Han identity was not the only nationalist narrative during the late Qing, it had nonetheless "deeply influenced the historical discourse throughout the twentieth century" and directly challenged the multiethnic "state nationalism" articulated by others, notably the reformers who took a far less radical view.[87]

Through an analysis of the writings and statements of the Han intellectuals, we are able to identify the historical development, along with the racial, cultural, and political dimension, of Han-centrism. As a form of hypernationalism, Han-centrism looks outward and responds to foreign stimuli, as perceived exploitation and victimization by foreign powers, be it the Manchu, the West, or Japan, has produced cultural narratives of humiliation, weakness, and shame and, as a result, the need to reestablish China's rightful position in the world. Furthermore, by taking the social Darwinian worldview where racial revolution is needed to bolster against external threats within the larger struggle for supremacy, Han-centrism is able to reproduce a distinct form of Han racism that clearly delineates an us (Han) versus them (the non-Han).

This racial belief system developed by Han intellectuals during the late Qing dynasty to oppose the Manchu and other foreign powers still matters in that it continues to be revived time after time by the Chinese elite to achieve political objectives.[88] With this in mind, the next chapter addresses the role Han-centrism played during the Mao period and the ways in which it continues to shape Chinese society today, particularly the relationship between the Han and certain minority groups in the country.

3 Han-Centrism in Chinese History and Today

The greatest force is common blood.

—Sun Yat-sen, *The Three Principles of the People*, 1927

Only in the late nineteenth century did the Chinese
learn that civilization had a plural.

—S.C.M. Paine, *The Sino-Japanese War of 1894–1895*, 2003

Nationalism serves myriad functions for a state's population and elites. In particular, as scholars have demonstrated, national history provides the people of a nation with "the false unity of a self-same."[1] In this sense, Benedict Anderson described the nation as an "imagined community." However, when studying the dynamics of national identity in modern China, we first have to ask who is doing the imagining and what internal and external influences are shaping the narratives of the nation, or what Prasenjit Duara aptly calls "nation views." This is a complex topic that requires deep exploration because Chinese nationalism is not invariable. Rather, as Yongnian Zheng correctly notes, "It has been repeatedly reconstructed in accordance with changing domestic priorities and international circumstances and is thus in a state of flux."[2]

Scholars have given much attention to the rise of ultranationalism in China since the 1989 protests in Tiananmen Square.[3] They are right to do so, as such aggressive sentiment has greatly shaped relations with Japan and the West, as well as the treatment of ethnic minorities within the country.[4] To explain the manifestations of this form of nationalism and its implications for international politics, this chapter addresses two major transformations of Chinese nationalism since the establishment of the People's Republic of China in 1949. The Chinese nationalism that once defined Mao Zedong's China has been replaced with a form of ethnic nationalism, according to Ming-yan Lai, that focuses inward and looks to the past in a "search for roots" (*xungen* [寻根]).[5] This emphasis on history and the roots of Han-ness within ethnic nationalist narratives has unleashed an aggressive Han-centrism that continues to shape the relationship between the Han and ethnic minorities in Chinese society as well as China's approach to foreign affairs.

Nationalism under Maoism

During Mao's rule (1949–76), nationalism was deeply ideological and based primarily on Marxism-Leninism.[6] Drawing largely from Communist ideology, this earlier form of nationalism was fiercely anti-imperialist and sought to escape China's Century of Humiliation by reasserting Chinese exceptionalism in the face of western hegemony. Within this nation view, China has been a victim of foreign oppression and aggression since the First Opium War of 1839. However, it was not so much China's defeat by foreigners that caused this humiliation, but rather the overturning of a long history of Sinocentrism in which imperial China was considered to be the center of the known world and a "tribute system" defined China's foreign relations with its neighbors.[7] According to Geremie Barmé, there is the belief held by many of the Chinese political elite that "the world (that is, the West) owes China something" and "past humiliations are often used as an excuse to demand better treatment from the West."[8]

To reclaim its rightful destiny and moral superiority, Mao's China drew from Communist ideology to produce a national identity defined by revolutionary Sinocentrism, or Tianxiaism, which argued for solidarity among the Chinese people in opposition to western imperialism. On this point, Douglas Howland argues: "In Mao's eyes, although the civilization of the Han Nationality most defined the civilization of the Chinese nation, all of China's nationalities were united as collective victims of imperialism and equal in their striving to shake off foreign oppression."[9]

Mao used similar rhetoric to make appeals of solidarity among "oppressed nations," and the PRC began building relationships with Africa and other Third World countries.[10] In this sense, Sinocentrism could be partially recovered. China was no longer the great power of the "known world," but it could become the center of the Third World and the great champion of anti-imperialism.

As Jian Chen argues, an age-old Chinese ethnocentrism and universalism penetrated Beijing's revolutionary policies and rhetoric of Third World solidarity. In particular, within the context of Sino-Vietnamese relations during the Cold War, the PRC demanded that Hanoi recognize China's moral superiority with the intention of creating "a modern version of the relationship between the Central Kingdom and its subordinate neighbors." When the Vietnamese refused, the Chinese "found it necessary to 'punish' their former comrades in order to defend their heavily wounded sense of superiority," resulting in "the final collapse of the 'alliance between brotherly comrades.'"[11]

This form of Chinese ethnocentrism, sometimes referred to as the "great Han chauvinism," profoundly shaped the PRC's vision of Han leadership within the struggle against western imperialism. Most telling are the arguments put forth by Li Weihan, chairman of the Nationalities Affairs Commission, on the role of the Han in China's self-determination. He argued, "In its long history, China had already become a Han-centric, unified, and multi-nationality state; the struggle against imperialism, feudalism, and bureaucratic capitalism required unity of all nationalities of China." In addition, "The Chinese revolution had to be led by the proletariat, a class that did not exist with minority nationalities, and therefore these peoples' separation from the Han would mean their deprivation of sound leadership."[12]

While Mao often spoke of the threat of unfettered Han chauvinism to the establishment of a multicultural Chinese society and warned of its pervasiveness in the CCP, Han-centrism could not be easily removed from Chinese socialism and its concept of the sovereign nation.[13] As Howland notes, "Mao's commitment to revolution relied on an imperialist principle and practice of the state, and deferred the question of the self-determination of autonomous regions until a future time when imperialism was crushed."[14] Until that time, minority nationalities would be transformed to meet the larger interests of Chinese socialism, which in turn required that they give up their claims to self-determination and instead follow the "sound leadership" of the Han in the revolutionary struggle of the world proletariat.

For Mao, China would be a vast nation comprising many nationalities, and those that resisted this vision were accused of actively preventing socialist development in China and supporting the "bourgeoisie in its exclusive domination of the state."[15] Furthermore, according to Morris Rossabi, the Communist leadership asserted that ethnic minorities would be protected under socialism and, as a result, would quickly recognize "the inherent superiority of socialism (as earlier they had acknowledged the splendor of traditional Chinese civilization and come to be transformed) and eventually integrate into Han culture."[16]

Despite the call on ethnic minorities to join the Han in the fight against imperialism, many of the political elite viewed the non-Han minority groups as backward and inferior, requiring Han tutelage to transform them into proletarian supporters of revolutionary socialism.[17] Through the process of eroticization and othering, Rossabi argues that the government "veered from professed concern for, or at least benign neglect toward, the minorities' unique cultures and beliefs to repression of their religions, language, cultures, and practices."[18] As a result, Han chauvinism lingered within government policies throughout the Maoist period, particularly with regard to national minorities and relations with neighboring countries.

From Communist Ideology to Ethnic (Han) Nationalism

Since the political and economic reforms of the early 1980s, Chinese policy makers and intellectuals, increasingly concerned with confronting western economic and military power, have abandoned the ideologically driven nationalism of the Cold War in favor of a new narrative of the nation that better suits China's changing role in international politics.[19] As the works of Jonathan Unger and Perry Link show, the demise of the Maoist ideology at this time produced a "crisis of faith" and a "thought vacuum" within the inner core of Chinese political and intellectual life.[20] The debate around China's "core problem" was not so much about finding a new political ideology to replace Maoism but rather a crisis of faith in Chinese culture, particularly among the political elite who were concerned with mobilizing a younger generation in support of new national interests while simultaneously preventing an outgrowth of cultural nihilism.[21]

To achieve this, Chinese nationalism would become less ideological and more Sinocentric, drawing primarily from Confucianism and ideals rooted in nativism and chauvinism to redeem past humiliations and regain international power.[22] These ideals were not imported solely from the West or completely new to China. Rather, these were Sinocentric beliefs that date back to imperial China and have since influenced Chinese political thought. This belief in Chinese exceptionalism is "an essential part of the worldview of the Chinese government and many intellectuals . . . [and] can also provide the ingredients for the supposed construction of Chinese theories of international relations that both policy makers and analysts inside China see as in dire need."[23] In sum, as has been recognized by many students of Chinese national identity, it has always involved many elements, and at alternative periods in China's history various elements and expressions have been emphasized by the government.[24]

Promoting Chinese Nationalism through Education Campaigns

To foster this sense of exceptionalism, the political elite, including Jiang Zemin, former general secretary of the Chinese Communist Party (CCP), have supported a nationalist discourse that emphasizes national spirit (*minzhu jingshen* [民主精神]), patriotism (*aiguozhuyi* [爱国主义]), and Chinese civilization (*Zhongguo wenming* [中国文明]).[25] To instill patriotism and xenophobia among the younger generations, the CCP has implemented a patriotic education campaign.[26]

At the core of this campaign of reshaping collective memory is a whitewashing of modern Chinese history, that is to say, a strategy of "misremembering the past" accompanied by historical narratives of "chosen glory" and "chosen trauma."[27] In these narratives, the crimes of the Mao era, the death and destruction of the Cultural Revolution, are absent, and the story of how Mao and the ruling party saved the Chinese people from the imperialism of barbarous foreigners, most notably the Japanese, is center stage. However, this "victor narrative," which defined the Mao period, has been more recently combined with another narrative that emphasizes Chinese suffering at the hands of foreign "devils."[28] Since the early 1990s, the government has attempted to promote this narrative by requiring that all school textbooks be revised to reflect this victimization theme, which blames the West for China's problems.[29]

The government draws heavily from history to refashion a national identity to meet the economic and political needs of a rapidly changing society. According to Zheng Wang, there are three core components of Chinese memory that underlie the government's patriotic campaigns and nationalist rhetoric: emergency and urgency, Chinese suffering at the hands of foreigners, and tensions with countries that have had historically bad relations with China, such as Japan and the West. The history and memory underlying the patriotic education, makes possible a shared identity that unites the people under the banner of redemption for past wrongs caused by external forces during the Century of Humiliation and resistance to continued "bullying" from the West.[30]

The government's objective here is quite simple: distract the Chinese people from the failures of the CCP, such as the notorious 1989 Tiananmen massacre and growing public concern over political corruption, by promoting patriotism among the younger generations that fosters an "us versus them" mentality.[31] According to the CCP Central Committee's education campaign, the intent is "to inspire national spirit, enhance national cohesiveness, set up national self-esteem and pride, reinforce and develop the broadest patriotic united front."[32] Such an understanding can also be seen in the teaching agenda set by the Ministry of Education for high school history courses. It captures our point well: "Chinese modern history is a history of humiliation that China had been gradually degenerated into a semi-colonial and semi-feudal society." Yet "it is also a history that Chinese people strived for national independence and social progress, persisted in their struggle of anti-imperialism and anti-feudalism, and was also the history of the success of New-Democratic Revolution under the leadership of the CCP."[33]

This attempt by the CCP to rewrite collective memory through education campaigns and the use of propaganda in textbooks has been challenged by the influx of western values and ideals within Chinese academic institutions. Acknowledging the growth of non-Chinese values on college campuses, the CCP has started to crack down on the spread of ideological material that challenges the victimization narrative and the government's legitimacy.[34] Along these lines, the government has banned academic research and coursework on seven "western" topics: universal values, civil society, citizens' rights, freedom of the press, benefits of capitalism, the independence of the judiciary, and mistakes made by the CCP.[35]

Despite the country's embrace of capitalism, socialism is the only western ideology considered by the government to be acceptable, with the call for new guidelines that require the "country's higher education institutions to prioritize the teaching of Marxism, ideological loyalty to the party, and the views of President Xi Jinping."[36] Viewing colleges and universities as ideological fronts in the war of ideas against the West, Education Minister Yuan Guiren called for the "Four Nevers" in the management of textbooks:

> NEVER let textbooks promoting western values enter our classes; NEVER allow speeches that slander the leadership of the Communist Party of China and smear socialism appear in our classes; NEVER allow speeches that violate the country's Constitution and laws prevail in university and college classes; NEVER allow teachers to vent their personal grudges or discontent while teaching to pass negative ideas to their students.[37]

This guidance is significant because of the traditional role that textbooks play in nationalist education for a country's youth. Unlike in the West, where other educational narratives would ensure that nationalism is tempered by an understanding of a country's past mistakes and profound faults, this is far less likely to happen in the Chinese educational system. One result of this is the relatively unfettered rise of ethnic nationalism among the elites and youth in China.

The Rise of Han Nationalism

With the emergence of China in global and regional politics, the PRC has pursued a two-pronged approach described as state-led nationalism—the establishment of a strong homogeneous identity with an assertive national self-awareness—and ethnic (Han) nationalism—the creation of a community that shares a common history, culture, and language.[38] Mostly this strategy has worked because the concepts of nation and state have been vaguely defined, yet nonetheless intertwined, in China since the Qing period.[39] What we see today is the CCP seeking to maintain legitimacy, making appeals to ethnic (Han) nationalist interests, *and* promoting patriotism and national identity by emphasizing China's long history and the country's disempowerment during the Century of Humiliation.[40]

However, the by-product of the state-led campaigns is not only a widespread cultural nationalism that overwhelmingly pervades Chinese society but also a growing number of "angry youth" who are helping fuel the rise of hypernationalism.[41] The CCP's emphasis on victimization and call to regain China's central role in international relations has gained a great deal of support within the growing populist nationalist movement from below, which perceives western criticism of Chinese domestic and foreign policies as bullying and an attempt to hinder China's return to great power status.[42] In fact, others have already noted the use of the internet by the angry youth to mobilize fellow nationalists in protest against perceived adversaries of the country, most notably the U.S. bombing of the Chinese embassy in Belgrade in 1999 and the 2005 protests against Japan.[43]

At the forefront of this movement are Han nationalists articulating their own counterclaims and voicing their right to participate in Chinese politics.[44] These aggressive nationalist counterclaims are attempts to shape the CCP's rewriting of collective memory, as well as to influence the position China takes in regional and global politics.[45] Such populist (Han-centric) nationalism can easily be found in the numerous "historical books" and novels that portray imperial China as benevolent and more advanced than the West and the need to reestablish the powerful position in international affairs that has been wrongly taken from the Chinese people.

For example, popular nationalist books like *Those Happenings in the Ming Dynasty* (2010), *Stories of the Two Song Dynasties* (2009), and *Memories of the Late Qing Dynasty* (2007) emphasize Han Chinese heroism, power politics, and social Darwinism, the failure of the cultural traditions of the neighboring countries, and the importance of territorial expansion through colonialism to revitalize China.[46] Moreover, these narratives have accompanied the growth of a "Greater China" nationalism, which calls for the preservation of China's territorial integrity at any cost.[47] Most important, within these historical novels, the aggressive nationalism of the anti-Manchu radicals is reproduced, as many of these accounts highlight Han supremacy and the Han-barbarian distinctions that made possible the Hanzu identity during the late Qing dynasty.

Furthermore, throughout the Chinese internet, young nationalists are demanding that China regain its regional dominance, as evinced in the tributary system that defined the dynastic period. According to this understanding, not only are Taiwan, Tibet, the Xinjiang Uighur Autonomous Region (XUAR), and Hong Kong part of "Greater China," but so are the islands and shoals of the South China Sea—anything within the "Nine-Dash Line." For the most extreme, even parts of Korea are included, specifically the territory of the ancient proto-Korean Kingdom of Goguryeo, 37 BC–AD 668.[48] As Peter Gries points out, this territorial claim has more to do with national identity, specifically defining the in-group and Chinese superiority ("big brother status") than political, economic, or security reasons.[49]

When China's president, Xi Jinping, claims that certain territories, such as the islands in the South China Sea, have been China's "since ancient times," he is effectively tapping into a deeply rooted memory of humiliation and exploitation that makes up Han identity.[50] Therefore, it is no surprise that young Chinese cybernationalists have responded to The Hague's recent decision to reject China's territorial claims with a militaristic video entitled *South China Sea Arbitration: Who Cares?*[51] The angry youth have bought into Xi's historical allusions and are united by a strong Han-centric identity and the patriotic desire to reassert Chinese civilization by reclaiming what outsiders have unfairly taken.

The online presence (blogs, chat rooms, and posts) of the angry youth and their demands for a more assertive China that looks more like Putin's

Russia and less like the United States has grown significantly over the years.[52] While the Chinese government's control of cyberspace is fairly efficient, especially with removing content deemed threatening to the CCP's legitimacy, "patriotic anger" on the Chinese internet remains one of the safe topics that the government tolerates and even encourages at times.[53]

As a result, hand in hand with the rise of new historical narratives have been an increasing number of popular nonfiction books calling for a more assertive and aggressive China. Books like *China Can Say No* (1996), *Unhappy China* (2008), and, most notably, Liu Mingfu's *China Dream* (2015) convey the Party's new victimization narrative and call for assertive foreign policies in the region and toward the United States, which is considered to be hindering China's rise. These writings represent an attempt to participate in Chinese politics by redefining Chinese nationalism and China's worldview. For example, these concerns have been popularized recently through a widely circulated essay by Zhou Xiaoping, a noted Chinese blogger, entitled "Nine Knockout Blows in America's Cold War against China."[54] In many of his posts, Zhou, using the victimization narrative, accuses the West of robbing, slaughtering, and brainwashing the Chinese through a campaign of "shame" and "slander." He also states that American culture is eroding the moral foundation and self-confidence of the Chinese people.[55]

Moreover, James Leibold captures this sentiment in a recent study of Han cybernationalism. His analysis of the online blogs and commentaries of Han nationalists claiming to be amateur historians found a number of radical arguments on the need to establish "a pure Han state with an unsullied Han culture at its core" and conspiracy theories about "how minority elite are teaming up with foreign forces to split China and undermine its national interests." Through their emphasis on the "brutal racial oppression" carried out by the Mongols and Manchus, historical enemies of the Han Chinese, these nationalists are tapping into the social Darwinian worldview of Han-centrism. As Leibold notes, "For Han nationalists . . . only those who actively defend and fight for Han cultural integrity can be considered great, and it is these patriotic 'martyrs' that they seek to immortalize on the fluid technoscapes of the Internet."[56]

Some scholars have already begun to investigate this relationship between the CCP and the populist movement. Philip Pan argues that "the government has grown expert at . . . rallying nationalist sentiment to its side," in turn greatly enhancing the Party's reputation.[57] Along similar lines, Gilbert Rozman writes: "The [Chinese] leadership has skewed debate over the symbols of sovereignty and national identity in ways that fuel intense reactions among a vocal part of the population." He continues, "Treating the temporal dimension as a mix of unvarnished pride in the fruits of Sinocentrism and exaggerated humiliation at the price of weakness, they have produced a narrative relatively unmitigated by conflicting themes."[58] Just as the Han intellectuals of the late Qing dynasty realized the importance of a strong racial consciousness to unify the people during the Xinhai Revolution, the CCP has found that playing the Han-centrism card is effective in mobilizing the population in opposition to those domestic and international actors considered threats to China's national interests.

President Xi Jinping was quick to endorse Zhou Xiaoping as "positive energy."[59] Compared with Deng Xiaoping's policy of "hide brightness, cherish obscurity" or Hu Jintao's "continuously keep a low profile and proactively get some things done," Xi is more overtly embracing the populist movement and its critique of the West.[60] Similar to the nationalist narratives discussed earlier, the ideological core of Xi's administration—China Dream—emphasizes the need to search for the roots of China's greatness in order to put the country back on the road to revival.[61] Because Xi fears that western political and economic ideas will undermine the power of the Chinese state, he appears to be resurrecting past glories to rejuvenate China.[62] Most notable is his recent emphasis on Confucianism as China's "native culture" and the importance of Confucius Institutes as a way to counterbalance western ideals.[63]

Reproducing Han-Centrism

In many ways, Xi's China Dream feeds into the narrative of Chinese exceptionalism, specifically the nostalgia of the dynastic period and the 1911 Xinhai Revolution, and national heroes like Sun Yat-sen.[64] For cybernationalists like Zhou Xiaoping and his fellow netizens, the Xinhai Revolution represents national awakening and serves as a model of how the Chinese (Han) people successfully overthrew foreign influence (the Manchu) that prevented their growth and prosperity.[65]

With this outgrowth of ethnic nationalism from above and below, we are witnessing the rise of Han-centric beliefs obsessed with the roots of Chinese weakness. It identifies pernicious foreign influences as the cause of China's downfall in the past and the obstacle to regaining its position of power in international relations.[66] The "foreigners" in this modern narrative are not just westerners but also internal foreigners, such as the various ethnic minorities within the country.

In particular, according to Chew and Wang, is the "claim that the real culprit that had prevented historical China from progressing into modernity was a non-Han ethnic group (the Manchus)."[67] Implicit in this is the argument that, had it not been for Manchu rule, China would have modernized, matched the West, and avoided colonization. Within this narrative, China and the Chinese people at large must once again embrace traditional social thoughts, religious beliefs, language, literature, and the like. As Chew and Wang point out, this cultural conservative discourse is not found solely among academics and the political elite but also reflects public concern and lay knowledge.

Despite the PRC's call for multiculturalism, Chinese ethnic nationalism has a Han-centric dimension, which claims that "the Han culture is the world's most advanced and its race is one of the strongest and most prosperous."[68] Furthermore, "The interests of the Han race are equivalent to the interests of China as a whole and the welfare of its people."[69] In this sense, what differentiates Han-centrism from state-led nationalism in general is the emphasis on race and culture, such that the Chinese nation (*guojia* [国家]) is believed to be the home of the Han people and the revival of Han culture is required for China's continued development.

While this Han-centric narrative runs counter to the government's "official" multicultural nationalism in which all fifty-six ethnic groups make up the nation, this understanding of Han exceptionalism as distinctly Chinese is well entrenched within the historical memory evoked by the political elite through patriotic education campaigns, revisionist historical novels, and widely read blog commentaries.[70]

In other words, Han-centrism may be understood as a form of hyper-nationalism which claims that the Han are racially purer, following social Darwinist thinking, than other peoples, and the Han way of life is superior to that of other cultural groups. In this view, Han culture is considered to be hardworking, disciplined, patriotic, and modest (conservative in behavior and dress), while the ethnic minorities of the country, or the more recent Africans working or studying in China, are seen as essentially the opposite—lazy, exotic, sexualized, undisciplined, and culturally backward.[71] This racialized understanding of the ethnic groups inside and outside the country can be seen as an example of what Jing Lin calls the "great Han mentality," which forms the basis of a deeply rooted discriminatory bias against the non-Han.[72]

While this mentality has a long history in Chinese racial thought, Reza Hasmath argues that the PRC, since its early days, has "reinforced the image of Han superiority by intertwining it into a Marxist ideology of progress." He adds, "Recognized minority nationalities were categorized according to five major modes of production: primitive, slave, feudal, capitalist, and socialist. The Hans were ranked the highest on this scale, reinforcing the Han idea that minorities are 'backward' and perpetuating the Communists' portrayal of Hans as the 'vanguard' of the people's revolution." With respect to ethnic minorities, they were "encouraged to follow the Han example."[73] In this sense, through a racial categorization,

Han-centric nationalism places China within a social Darwinian world, one that resurrects "martial values that in the past had led its dynasties to expand territorially across Asia" and emphasizes that "every event in China's 'neighborhood' involving other actors is a potential challenge to China's status and thus must be met with an immediate response."[74]

Manifestations of Han-Centrism in Chinese National Identity

When we consider China's treatment of its indigenous ethnic minorities, we begin with the recognition that there are fifty-five minorities in China. Yet in daily life, most Chinese do not come into contact with many of these groups, since they are on the periphery, both literally and metaphorically. Nonetheless, within Chinese society there is a clear hierarchy among them.

The two most important minority groups are the Uighurs and Tibetans. Broadly, the relationships between the Han Chinese and these minorities are very bad.[75] The Han resent the affirmative action policies in support of the Uighurs and Tibetans, their lack of gratitude for what China has provided, and what is seen as their rebellious nature. Some minority groups see the Han as occupiers of their ancestral lands, abusive and contemptuous toward them, and bent on the extermination of their way of life and national identities, while the rest of the world tacitly accepts it.

Our discussion begins with recognition that the presence of Han-centrism in Chinese national identity is well ensconced. The Party's position was captured by Vice Premier Hui Liangyu in 2007 when he stated, "The minority nationalities cannot be separated from the Han, and the Han cannot be separated from the nationalities."[76] Given that perspective and approach to minority issues, it is no surprise that minority rights are in practice neglected by the government.

As mentioned earlier, Han-centrism can be found all over the Chinese internet, especially within popular nationalist blogs like Zhou Xiaoping's. Chew and Wang cite the following expression of this powerful sentiment:

"We are looking forward to Han ethnic group's invigoration and China's gaining of wealth and power!" From that bold start the author continues, "Alas, I feel sorry that our countrymen's sense of belonging to the Han ethnic group is too weak! In order to awake the Han spirit in everyone and to raise ethnic pride, we need to popularize the classical culture of the Han ethnic group."[77]

While the Han-centric narrative considers the Manchu to be the historical culprit, other ethnic groups in the country today are also seen as threats to China's reawakening, particularly those that challenge Han or Sinocentric traditions and resist acculturation.[78] For example, Uighurs, in particular, are all too often targets of Han-centrism. Such discrimination is intensified by what Enze Han (2010) refers to as "rigid group boundaries" between the Han Chinese and the Uighur. The perception of the Uighur as "backward" and "lazy," along with interethnic tensions due to linguistic and cultural differences, has made it difficult for many to find employment in the urban job market. As Han notes, "Many job advertisements explicitly state that only Han Chinese can apply."[79] And as clashes between the Han settlers and Uighur separatists in Xinjiang intensify and become more violent, such attitudes toward the Uighurs will undoubtedly grow, especially with the Chinese government's ongoing crackdown on some Islamic practices in the region.[80]

Animosity between Han and Uighurs came to a head in July 2009 when more than two hundred people were confirmed killed during rioting, principally in Urumqi. The grievances of the Uighur population of Xinjiang have been exacerbated by mass immigration from other parts of China, which is part of Beijing's Sinification campaign to turn the majority Uighur population into a minority in Xinjiang by resettling Han Chinese. In May 2010, the Communist Party held a Xinjiang Work Conference and concluded that "the fundamental way to resolve the Xinjiang problem is to expedite development in Xinjiang."[81]

This modernization comes at a cost and is believed to be an attempt to destroy Uighur culture under the guise of development, as Kashgar's transformation into a Special Economic Zone entailed the demolition of the historic old city. This was done under the auspices of making it earthquake-proof and to improve access to public services. However, Uighurs interpreted it as further destruction of their cultural heritage and part of Beijing's effort to erode the collective memory and cultural identity of the Uighur people.[82]

As a result, there has been an increase in violence in the province, particularly in the south, where Uighurs remain a majority of the population. In July 2011 a group of Uighurs stormed a police station in Hotan, a city south of Kashgar, having earlier attacked a nearby tax office. In early August, local media reported that trouble flared in Kashgar when one or two car bombs misfired in public spaces before men armed with knives hijacked a vehicle and drove it into a crowd, killing eight and injuring twenty-seven. A similar incident occurred a day later and was directed at a largely Han crowd. December 2011 marked another incident in Guma county in the Hotan prefecture, and two months later, on February 28, 2012, another stabbing incident took place and thirteen Uighur men attacked passersby.[83] Finally, in June 2012, the government raided a religious school in Hotan, injuring several children. Later that month, six Uighur men attempted to hijack a flight leaving from Hotan to call attention to anti-Uighur discrimination before they were overpowered by the crew and passengers.[84]

The fundamental problem remains that since the 2009 riots, the Uighur situation is not better. The prosperity that was meant to be generated by the 2010 Xinjiang work conference plan has not yet trickled down, with many of the large projects in limbo as the government has difficulty convincing investors that the province is a good investment opportunity.[85] While the infrastructure in the province has been rapidly and effectively upgraded, making travel around the province easier, and the "paired" provinces have spent considerable money in Xinjiang, it apparently is not having the desired effect of reducing discontent there.

Social dissatisfaction remains high on all sides. Complaints made by many Uighurs are consistent: they see Han overwhelming the province and a lack of economic opportunities for Uighurs. According to Alim Seytoff of the Uighur American Association, "the whole idea" behind Beijing's efforts "is to secularize the Uighur people."[86] It also marginalizes them in their own province. Yet the concerns are reciprocal, if not existential for the Han. Common Han remarks are fear of going into Uighur areas due to growing concerns of crime and violence.

The development challenges facing Xinjiang are exacerbating the long-standing ethnic divisions that plague the province. The repeated incidents of low-level violence directed by the Uighurs at the Han may have outside links and be inspired by jihadist beliefs, but in most cases they are more likely caused by local explosions of rage and are not the start of an effective revolutionary movement directed at the government. However, since October 2012 there have been reports that Chinese Muslim separatists are fighting in Syria alongside ISIS, al Qaeda, and associated movements, all of which can only be alarming for Beijing.[87]

In Beijing's view, this has legitimized the Chinese government's ongoing crackdown on some Islamic practices in the region.[88] These include restricting the ability of Uighur to acquire a passport, banning twenty-nine common Muslim baby names, "irregular" beards, religious education and marriage ceremonies, and "words and actions" that the Chinese government may consider to be promoting extremism, all as part of the government's efforts to chip away at the cultural foundation of the Uighurs.[89]

Along similar lines, since the revolutionary Sinocentrism of the Mao era, China has attempted to take a leadership role in Africa. An increasing number of Africans are coming to China to study, while many Chinese merchants have migrated to African countries in search of work. Associated with this is a spike in anti-African racism on college campuses in China, suggesting that discourses of race are a central underlying component of Han-centric nationalism and "racism with Chinese characteristics will keep growing as China continues to be a global power."[90]

In fact, for many of the Africans studying and working in China, such overt discrimination is all too common.[91] According to M. Dujon Johnson, racism is "prevalent, unchecked, and widespread in Chinese society. These complaints by African students ranged from impolite and racist statements by Chinese citizens to threats, intimidation, and physical assaults." He also writes that "the Chinese are clear that Africans and African Americans are not very desirable as a people and they will be grudgingly tolerated in Chinese society. It is not an exaggeration to state that most Chinese would rather all Blacks return home to Africa even if they are not Africans."[92]

Through an analysis of this portrayal of the non-Han, we can begin to understand how Han nationalists shape the ongoing debate around national identity as they struggle to redefine the Chinese state and who belongs. As Kai-wing Chow contends, historically Chinese intellectuals have looked to the Other, the generalized enemy, to narrate the Chinese nation.[93] A similar process is playing out today: the PRC's attempt to rewrite collective memory to support China's political and economic rise in international politics has reawakened a Han-centrism that holds an extremely racialized worldview.

Furthermore, xenophobia, defined here as fear and contempt of foreigners, plays a significant role in the Han-centric narrative.[94] According to Ben Xu, the Chinese government elicits xenophobia to unify the population against international criticism and pressure by portraying foreign influence as a threat to the Chinese way of life, be it outside accusations of human rights abuses or the dangers that western (i.e., alien) values, cultural heritage, modes of knowledge, and vision of history pose to Chinese exceptionalism.[95]

For example, after a young Han nationalist slapped intellectual Yan Chongnian in October 2008, there was a shared consensus in blogs, chat rooms, and message boards that Yan deserved to be "beaten like an old dog" because his sympathy for minority rights made him a "bastard Manchu worm" and a "Tartar coated" Han.[96] These racial slurs are particularly insightful to the racism and marginalization associated with Han-centrism, in which the other ethnic identities in the country, Manchu and Tartar in this case, become derogatory and belittling terms.

Another example of how Han-centrism is attempting to shape constructions of race and Chineseness can be seen in the 2009 cyberspace debate over the national identity of Chinese television show contestant Lou Jing, a woman of Chinese and African American descent. As Robeson Frazier and Lin Zhang point out, the xenophobia and racism of this form of nationalism has a strong antiblack discourse associated with it, such that Lou Jing's dark complexion and her claim to Chinese ethnicity became a point of contention for many netizens. For most, Lou Jing's dark skin marked her as "black" and thus overrode her claims to Chinese nationality. According to nationalist bloggers, she had no legitimate connection to the Han ethnic lineage that defines the nation but rather was seen by many as a "black chimpanzee" and "black devil" that "polluted the larger Chinese national body."[97]

It may be easy to disregard the slapping of Yan Chongnian and the racial slurs against Lou Jing, as one might consider such sentiment as the nonsense and defamations commonly found throughout cyberspace. Numerous scholars of contemporary China have pointed out the importance of the internet in the construction of Chinese national identity. The revival of Han chauvinism found on online forums like *Baidu Tieba* [百度贴吧] is no exception. For example, forums on Han nationality and traditional Han culture (*Huaxia* [華夏]) include such topics as rejuvenating the great Han nationality and the importance of promoting traditional Han culture.[98]

Although it is difficult to empirically prove the pervasiveness of Han-centrism on the internet and in modern Chinese society, the research covered on Chinese nationalism above suggests that these racial beliefs and opinions matter for the reconstruction of national identity. In fact, not only does China engage the world through social media but Chinese cyberspace also serves as an outlet for political venting and identity formation that have contributed to "the reemergence of nationalist consciousness."[99]

Furthermore, through this revival of Han identity and desire to reclaim Han greatness, the Chinese government is able to use the strong ethnocentrism and xenophobia of Han-centrism to promote what Isabelle Côté refers to as "Han regional minority mobilization." To support the political mobilization of Han Chinese settlers in XUAR, the PRC not only ignores the growing Han aggression toward the Muslim majority, arresting far more Uighur than Han during outbreaks of violence, but the government has also created the circumstances under which the Han settlers migrate to the XUAR in the first place. According to Côté, "by promulgating Han-friendly policies in the effort to persuade them to stay in Xinjiang permanently," the Chinese government responds favorably to Han demands and fosters "a political discourse justifying Han settler presence in minority areas."[100]

While the number of Han settlers in Xinjiang has grown in recent years, the mobilization of Han Chinese by the government in minority-dominated areas is not new. During the Mao period, the government, in the form of a civilizing mission, sent down (*xia fang* [下放]) millions of young urban Han Chinese into minority areas to "build a socialist countryside" and teach the ethnic communities the advanced Han way of life.[101] In this sense, the *xia fang* movement was an attempt at Sinicization by the government, and for the minorities, this meant attacks on the "'feudal nature' of many of their customs and religious practices, their languages, and the alleged extravagance of their traditional costumes."[102] Thus, since Mao, the mobilization of Han Chinese has been predicated on the chauvinism and nativism of Han-centrism and the attempt to rally the population under the discourse of revitalizing and defending Chinese exceptionalism.

What is more, the PRC refuses to accept such chauvinism and racism as a problem, as well as the overall aggressive nature of Han-centric nationalism. According to Barry Sautman, this failure to acknowledge and address the prevalence of ethnic prejudice in the country has been going on for many years, with high-profile political leaders such as Deng Xiaoping and Zhao Ziyang arguing that racism and ethnic discrimination have never existed in China and are instead problems that other countries face.[103] Of course, the PRC has formal constitutional protections for ethnic minority identities, cultures, and languages, and insists that Chinese identity is ethnically neutral and multicultural, while preaching harmony between China's many ethnic groups as part of its state-led patriotic campaigns and through the bureaucracy.[104] But despite these safeguards, the government continues to draw out the Han-centric sentiment deeply embedded within the population when some of these ethnic minorities challenge governmental policies or during territorial disputes with other countries in the region.[105]

The Treatment of Christians within China

Perhaps surprisingly, Chinese hypernationalism has had less of an impact on Christianity, particularly because the Catholic Church and Protestant dominations have been Sinified. Their practices are controlled or heavily influenced by the Communist Party, which ensures that Christian practices are in accord with its wishes, as well as the practices of the other officially recognized religions in China: Buddhism, Islam, Daoism, Catholicism, and Protestantism. At the same time, religious life in China has recovered from its suppression during the Maoist years.

China's Christian tradition dates from the early 1500s. The Portuguese and Dutch were the first to bring Christianity, and missionary zeal reached its peak in the early twentieth century. The relationship between Christianity and China is complicated with many reverses and considerable tension.[106] According to historian David Mungello, the Christians, especially the Jesuit order, were first welcomed into China and successful in converting prominent scholar-officials. "This success came through the conscious blending of Confucianism with Christianity while criticizing Buddhism and Daoism."[107] As Christian orders proliferated and more of the elite and lower classes were converted, the court's attitude began to change, and elements of Christian proselytizing were prohibited.

As a response, the Franciscans and Church lay groups began meeting in secret, which was unfortunate given the court's suspicion of secret societies. In the consideration of the court, they are linked to peasant uprisings, for which the societies provide organization around an ideology. The uprisings are nearly always aimed at the scholar-gentry class, who were viewed by the peasants as oppressors because they controlled the land and bureaucracy. Because of this hostility, the scholar-officials viewed secret societies with suspicion and enmity. "Like the secret societies, Christianity was often accused by the literati of subversive practices, such as prohibiting ancestor worship, meeting in small groups, using magical techniques to control followers, deceiving the people, and failing to observe customary distinctions of age and sex."[108]

Anti-Christian sentiment gradually began to grow, especially after the Manchu conquest of 1644, and as Mungello argues, Chinese ethnocentrism, chauvinism, and xenophobia became worse and Christianity was suppressed, though never eliminated.[109]

More recently, the relationship between Christianity and nationalism in modern Chinese history is equally difficult. At the peak of nationalist agitation in the mid-1920s, many radical Chinese began to believe that Christianity was a tool of western imperialism and that it was a narrow and intolerant faith. This was part of a larger reaction to religion; modern men did not need such superstitions. At the same time, others saw

Christianity as part of China's rebirth. Why should the religion not serve the same purpose in China as it had in the West, where it had given meaning to unsettled lives and steadiness through uncertain times for almost two thousand years? For China's Christians it was not difficult to see themselves as part of their country's salvation, in both a religious and secular sense, even if their opponents objected to it.

Today the government recognizes that religion is able to do many positive things in a society, such as support orphanages, and it acknowledges the need for people to have a religious grounding, since a moral framework may be lost in the demands of a market economy. The debate now is an echo of the one they had in the 1800s: how do they preserve the essence of what is Chinese in an era dominated by western ideas?[110]

The government is fearful of religion in the sense that uncontrolled religion might challenge Beijing's authority. The government has considerable fear of cults and the contagion of foreign ideas, especially following the Tiananmen Square massacre of 1989.[111] So, in order to be recognized, religions in China must be autonomous as interpreted by the government. That is, autonomy is defined as having no foreign missions, no foreign subsidy, and no interference from foreign ecclesiastics. Because of this, Beijing favors evangelical sects, as Guy Sorman writes: "The truth is that Protestants outnumber Catholics ten to one. But the Party finds it easier to deal with scattered evangelical groups than with an organized Catholic Church that receives its orders from outside. Between the Vatican and Yankee Protestantism, the Communist Party prefers the Americans."[112]

The result is a state church and an underground church in China. According to Mungello, the best thing that happened to Christianity in China is that Mao expelled the missionaries. This forced the churches to become fully Chinese. Contrary to what was often argued, "Christianity (along with Confucianism) had not died out in Communist China, but had gone underground. When it began to reemerge in the 1980s, it was far more Sinified than when it had been dominated by western missionaries and mission boards prior to 1951."[113] During the intervening years, it had deepened its roots in Chinese culture. Now, to the degree that there is tension, it is Chinese Christian versus Chinese non-Christian, which is very different than foreign missionary versus Chinese.

4 Implications of Han-Centrism for Chinese Foreign Policy and International Politics

> People are saying, "We've had bad people before. The whites were bad, the Indians were worse, but the Chinese are the worst of all."
> —Guy Scott, former head of the Patriotic Front Party in Zambia

In many respects, the United States today is in a situation similar to the one Nathan Leites of the Rand Corporation found himself in at the outset of the Cold War. At that time, the central question was how to understand and predict Soviet actions, and Leites developed what he termed the "operational code of the Politburo."[1] Scholars today face similar puzzlement when they attempt to analyze China.

The United States had few Sovietologists during the Cold War, but it has a legion of Sinologists who are tasked with analyzing and predicting Chinese behavior. Yet, for all of the writings of countless Sinologists, U.S. policy makers are still in doubt over Chinese motivations, as well as how the Chinese perceive the world.

As Aaron Friedberg wrote in his exceptional study of the future U.S. relationship with China, "The truth is that China is too important to be left to the China hands."[2] Indeed it is. Friedberg's insight underscores the importance of research into what are too often shared assumptions about China, and he calls attention to the reality that China does not

live up to international norms on identifying and combating hypernationalism in its society.

It is important that research is conducted by analysts who are outsiders to the "China community." They are thus free to critique Chinese
policies precisely because the government has no leverage over them and
so cannot punish or reward them as Beijing sees fit, and they are not
expected to share professional assumptions and common approaches to
the professional study of China.

Bringing domestic factors into the study of China's foreign relations
is empirically difficult given the informal mechanisms and the lack of
information available on decision-making processes, such as the degree
of influence that the military and bureaucratic factions have.[3] As a result,
we must start unpacking the black box of foreign policy decisions.[4]

Han-centrism appears to be promoted and reproduced at the top by
the political elite and at the bottom by nationalist elements like the angry
youth, settlers, bloggers, and those in the diaspora.[5] Beijing tolerates and,
in some cases, stirs up the hypernationalism when pressured by foreign
forces or by non-Han minority groups that are viewed as an obstacle to
the country's development.[6]

For example, during the 1999 anti-American protests following the
accidental bombing of China's embassy in Belgrade during the NATO
intervention in Yugoslavia, the government not only provided the "buses
to take students to foreign embassies and consulates" but also supplied
"the slogans that they should shout once they got there."[7] However, as
Zhao notes, the government eventually lost control over the protestors,
who became very suspicious of China's involvement in Belgrade.[8]

While the Chinese government appears to be playing a dangerous
game with Han-centrism, it has shown the ability to adapt to pressure
from below. James Reilly argues that China is a robust and flexible regime
that has adapted well to rapid growth.[9] His study of public opinion's
influence on Beijing's foreign policy reveals the government responding

to public opinion as well as shaping it. He suggests that the Chinese Communist Party combines tolerance and responsiveness with persuasion and repression. This "responsive authoritarianism" accounts for why the CCP has thrived since the end of the Cold War. It has developed a mechanism for tolerating sporadic instances of public emotion while maintaining its overall foreign policy trajectory.

This accounts for the Party's intermittent tolerance of popular protests and responsiveness to public pressures, as well as its subsequent crackdowns and policy reversals. It also accounts for the considerable consistency in Beijing's relationships with foreign governments. There were major protests against Indonesia in 1998, the United States in 1999, and Japan in 2010 and 2012. Following each instance, Chinese leaders moved quickly to mitigate the damage to bilateral relations, offering reassurances and working to stabilize bilateral ties. Instead of completely acceding to nationalist pressures for a more aggressive foreign policy, the CCP has developed an effective strategy for responding to outbursts of public anger on foreign policy. By making partial policy shifts or rhetorical gestures in the directions demanded by the public, Chinese leaders enable the release of anger and demonstrate a modicum of responsiveness to public opinion. Such shifts are generally part of a broader strategy of readjusting their overall foreign policy toward an approach that cools public anger, redirects the public's attention, and mitigates any diplomatic fallout resulting from following the dictates of an emotional public too closely.

By combining a diplomatic strategy designed to reshape the external environment with its considerable propaganda power to refocus attention, limit the flow of information, and project selective images to large segments of the public, the Party manages to end public mobilization without irreparable harm to foreign relations and without leaving behind a mass of dissatisfied citizens.

As previous research has shown, party-based regimes are able to avoid falling into foreign aggression as easily due to their ability to tolerate and respond to public anger in selective fashion.[10] It is this combination of toleration and repression that enables Chinese leaders to avoid ruin. The repeated eruption and temporary influence of popular protests in China in response to perceived slights to national pride signal not the emergence of an uncontrollable populace but rather the manifestation of policy makers' strategic and nuanced reaction to social pressures.

In a thoughtful study, Xi Chen makes a related argument. China is an example of a rare phenomenon. It is a strong authoritarian regime that has accommodated or facilitated widespread and routine popular collective action for a relatively long time. China has witnessed the most dramatic change in government-citizen interaction since the era of economic reform, with a great upsurge in collective protests beginning in the early 1990s. For Chen, this is due to the transition to a market economy, which relaxed the degree to which dissention would be permitted. Second, extensive economic transitions have engendered many grievances among large sections of the population. Third, the way ordinary people connect to the Party and government changed radically. With the abolition of collectivization in the countryside and the substantial decline of work units in urban areas, ordinary people have parted with the unit system of local control. According to Chen, "They have lost most of the benefits and security associated with the old system, but they have also been freed from" their dependence on local agents, which pushes them toward protest as a mechanism of influence.[11]

Naturally, external threats and crises assist the government. As Ji You explains, "Coping with an external enemy helps the Chinese government to reconstruct a defense culture useful for maintaining national unity. This is done in the name of patriotism." The people accept "that the nation faces an international challenge, which has served to draw the people toward the State." For example, following the Belgrade embassy bombing, China confronted "mounting domestic problems such as large-scale laying off of state workers and the widening gap between rich and poor." This required the government to develop "a striking slogan and an effective icon to rally the people," which it found "in national campaigns for patriotism."[12]

However, despite the CCP's past success with controlling and harnessing the population's anger and frustration, growing evidence suggests that Beijing's use of the nationalist card appears to be creating Stuart Kaufman's "symbolic politics trap."[13] At times the PRC struggles to put the nationalists back in their box as demonstrations spiral out of control both online and in the public sphere, harming China's diplomatic relations.[14]

One troubling example involves the racist and xenophobic comments found throughout the Chinese blogosphere during former U.S. secretary of state Condoleezza Rice's visit to Beijing in 2005. According to Chinese literary critic Liu Xiaobo [刘晓波], "Many stigmatized Rice as 'really ugly' . . . 'the ugliest in the world.' . . . 'I really can't understand how mankind gave birth to a woman like Rice.' . . . Some directly call Rice a 'black ghost,' a 'black pig,' . . . 'a witch' . . . 'rubbish of humans.'"[15] Additional remarks included: "How come the United States selects a female chimpanzee as secretary of state?"[16] Another blogger wrote: "I don't support racism, but this black ghost really makes people angry, the appearance of a little black [woman] who has made good."[17]

The vicious attack on Rice's race and gender is just one of many cases of Han nationalist outbursts online. While there are a number of liberal leaning commenters on sites like Weibo who condemn such racist and hypernationalist sentiment, they are often overshadowed by the more aggressive users, who actively disseminate anti-American and anti-Japanese rhetoric.[18]

As Thomas Christensen notes: "Apparently gone are the days when Chinese elites could ignore these voices. . . . Therefore, nationalist pundits and bloggers in China find allies in high places, and top government officials are nervous about countering this trend directly." He continues, "The result has been the creation of a dangerously stunted version of a free press, in which a Chinese commentator may more safely criticize government policy from a hawkish, nationalist direction than from a moderate, internationalist one"[19]

In fact, it appears that Han-centrism is beginning to co-opt Chinese foreign policy in that elites have been forced to move away from a pragmatic ("peaceful rise") view of international politics to a more aggressive and muscular approach. Some have already noted that due to its access to public media, the military has significant influence over specific foreign and diplomatic actions, such as territorial disputes with neighboring countries.[20] For example, although seldom explicitly found among China's top leaders, the notable exception being Liu Mingfu's *China Dream*, a growing number of low- and midlevel People's Liberation Army officers, such as Luo Yuan, a major general from the PLA Academy of Military Science, are embracing the populist nationalist narrative and advocating that military officers should be hawks, not doves, and show the sword whenever necessary.[21]

The growth of Han-centrism within the ranks of the PLA and the Ministry of Foreign Affairs appears to be a concern of the Xi administration and the reason behind Xi's push for China's new National Security Commission. David Lampton contends the NSC will allow Xi to "consolidate his personal sway on the domestic, foreign policy, and military realm," with a specific objective of controlling the "free-wheeling corruption and untethered military Hu Jintao had tolerated."[22] However, reining in the relatively autonomous security apparatus of China will require Xi to make inroads with the PLA, as opposed to simply overturning a fairly entrenched power structure.

Xi's influence over the PLA, according to James Mulvenon, is strengthened by his extensive political and military experience and knowledge of the operations at the highest levels of the bureaucratic system.[23] As a result, under the Xi administration, the PLA, which You Ji refers to as Xi's primary power base, seems to be playing a larger role in setting the strategic agenda.[24] This has become a concern because while not all Chinese military leaders are hawks, a larger number appear to be more nationalistic than their civilian counterparts, and they take a hardline stance on most security issues, especially those concerning territorial disputes and U.S. involvement in the region.[25] As Yawei Liu and Justine Zheng Ren note, Xi is using the PLA to consolidate power and actively "curtail internal corruption and prepare for war over the rising tensions of the East China Sea and the South China Sea."[26]

Furthermore, a strong Chinese military is a key component of Xi's goal of reviving nationalism. Acknowledging the changing nature of Chinese civilian-military relations, Jeremy Page submits: "Mr. Xi has made high-profile visits to army, air force, space program, and missile command facilities in his first 100 days in office, something neither of his two immediate predecessors did. He has taken personal control of China's military response to a newly inflamed territorial dispute with Japan." He has also "launched a campaign to enhance the military's capacity to 'fight and win wars.'"[27]

However, bureaucratic fragmentation within China's Central Military Commission has made "substantial room for myriad maritime security actors to push their own agendas," especially in the South China Sea, in turn posing a major challenge to Xi's attempt at top-down leadership over the PLA.[28] While there is civil-military consensus on certain aspects of Chinese foreign policy, such as territorial integrity, You Ji argues that agreement on the use of force remains unclear, especially within the context of the U.S. pivot to Asia.[29]

Fearing a national movement against the state, President Xi and many government officials may continue to pander to hawkish foreign policies of the PLA and the Ministry of Foreign Affairs to gain popularity and distract nationalists from questioning the political legitimacy of the CCP, while using such animus to sustain economic growth and confront security concerns. Since a historically weak and humiliated China is a central grievance in the Han-centric narrative, Han nationalists have rallied behind CCP hardliners and PLA hawks and pushed political and military leaders to take aggressive action against internal and external forces perceived as a threat to China's rise. In other words, as Minxin Pei asserts, "China's national experience and collective memory constitute a powerful force in foreign policy decision making."[30]

Moreover, considerable evidence suggests that nationalists are increasingly able to operate and mobilize independently of the government. Due to the outgrowth of nationalism, fueled by the angry youth and the proliferation of histories and novels with aggressive nationalist themes by "popular historians," the government appears to be losing its hegemony over the nationalist discourse and the rewriting of collective memory.

Han nationalists are shaping the Chinese government's view of international politics in two ways. First, their expectation is of a tribute system, just as China practiced diplomacy in the past—famously known to the West as *koutou* or *kowtow* [叩头]—in which it is quite clear who is superior and who is inferior. Indeed, a rather telling fact is that in the past, China never sent any ambassadors abroad; the rest of the world was expected to come to them. The same behavior may be found in modern-day China. Mao never visited any country other than the Soviet Union, and he did so only briefly.[31] As Lucien Pye explains, "The most pervasive underlying Chinese emotion is a profound, unquestioned, generally unshakable identification with historical greatness. . . . This is all so evident that they are hardly aware when they are being superior to others." Pye continues, "The Chinese see such an absolute difference between themselves and others that even when living in lonely isolation in distant countries they unconsciously find it natural and appropriate to refer to those in whose homeland they are living as 'foreigners.'"[32]

Second, there is an implicit racist view of international politics that is alien and anathema to western policy makers and analysts. Racist stereotypes are used to explain events. It would be unthinkable that a western political leader could do the same. This becomes particularly important in the Chinese message to the developing world: we do not care about your politics, and we mind our own business. Of course, they do not, and Chinese business practices in Africa are often reprehensible. However, the Chinese attitude allows them to anticipate a U.S. response.

In Chinese strategic thought, emphasis is placed on the psychological condition of one's own side and one's opponent.[33] In particular, a first strike or preemptive strategy will have a determinative psychological effect on the opponent that will, in turn, cause the opponent's withdrawal or collapse. As an eminent historian of Chinese strategic thought, Peter Boodberg, observed in 1930, the crux of the traditional Chinese battle narrative is psychological: battles are won and lost because something happens that causes the men on one side to lose their nerve and flee the battlefield.[34]

The psychological emphasis is a key component of Chinese warfare. Psychological effects are important in every confrontation, including a civil war between Chinese factions. However, the psychological aspect is seen a bit differently when China confronts non-Chinese. There is an assumption, often implicit, that the Chinese are superior.

This assumption is caused by the strong ethnocentrism at the heart of what it means to be Chinese. Noted historian of China S.C.M. Paine writes that the "Chinese made the a priori assumption that Chinese civilization was eternal, supreme, and predestined to triumph. They understood that Chinese dynasties had often been separated by decades of civil war, but they insisted that Chinese history was an unbroken cloth." They presented themselves "as guardians of a 5,000-year-old heritage of cultural continuity in contrast to the insipid attempts at civilization by the cultural parvenus inhabiting the rest of the globe."[35] Along similar lines, Odd Arne Westad argues: "The Chinese had a value system they called *Huayiguan* [华夷观], meaning—in a cultural context—'Chinese superior, others inferior.'" He continues: "Over centuries this world-view had influenced the Chinese eye in seeing other peoples and their behavior. As a form of cultural ethnocentrism, it was probably stronger at the time than any similar European phenomenon," in no small part "because it had been shared for half a millennium or more by large parts of the elites of China's immediate neighbors."[36]

The Chinese are said not only to share a common ancestry but also to derive from progenitors who, before the reign of the ancient Yellow Emperor, separated themselves from non–East Asians, becoming the "core of the yellow race."[37] Thus, due to religious-cultural and historical influences, strong Han nationalism remains a dominant social perspective and attitude. It allows the Chinese to easily define their worldview, to know who is in the "family" and who is the outsider, from whom they should expect support and from whom they should not. Such strong beliefs compel us to recognize that all things "Chinese" will generate the strongest emotional reactions. These attitudes were common in the past, explicitly made even when China had its period of doubt during the Century of Humiliation. However, policy makers and analysts should prepare for continually greater nationalistic, ethnocentric, and racist appeals as China becomes stronger.

Growing Chinese strength will breed overconfidence. This will be made worse by Han ethnocentrism and a sense of superiority rooted in a profound and dangerous conception of the modern world.[38] In particular, conflict could occur through a miscalculated "strategic manipulation of events," referred to as *shi* [势]. The correct interpretation of *shi* allows us to understand Deng Xiaoping's twenty-four-character instruction to Chinese officials as an archetype: "Observe carefully; secure our position; cope with affairs; hide our capabilities and bide our time; be good at maintaining a low profile; and never claim leadership."[39] The strategic objective of dominance is firm and unalterable but packaged in such a manner as to provoke the least resistance or effective counterbalancing coalition.

Understanding *shi* allows analysts to understand why the Chinese place great weight on intelligence gathering. One of the fundamental strategic goals of intelligence operations is being able to identify and shape events before they become sources of confrontation or contention.[40] With this strategy, the adversary can do nothing about the situation when he is confronted with it. The battle will be won before it is fought, and if the Chinese have done their homework, there will not be a battle in the first place. The Chinese seek to win without confrontation by placing the opponent in such a position that he withdraws of his own accord.

Shi also provides the Chinese with both the grounding and the flexibility for their policies. One core interest exists, and it is one that does not permit flexibility in intent: to advance China's fundamental interest of dominance. Once we move beyond this, we understand that everything else is flexible. The Chinese will change their policies as events develop. The implication is that China's policies will be hard to predict and may border on what seems to be impulsive, such as the dramatic intervention in the Korean War.

In addition, *shi* allows us to understand how the Chinese will work to undermine their adversaries in the expectation that they will be able to defeat their adversaries without direct confrontation and bring about their collapse from present conditions. However, if conflict does occur, the Chinese will seek to defeat their adversaries with asymmetric strategies and with surprise attacks. As Henry Kissinger writes:

> The strategist mastering *shi* is akin to water flowing downhill, automatically finding the swiftest and easiest course. A successful commander waits before charging headlong into battle. He shies away from an enemy's strength; he spends his time observing and cultivating changes in the strategic landscape. He studies the enemy's preparations and his morale, husbands resources and defines them carefully, and plays on his opponent's psychological weaknesses—until at last he perceives the opportune moment to strike the enemy at the weakest point. He then deploys his resources swiftly and suddenly, rushing "downhill"

along the path of least resistance, in an assertion of superiority that careful timing and preparation have rendered a fait accompli.[41]

Discerning *shi* properly allows analysts to grasp why the Chinese will place great emphasis on a bold, clever attack, as in 1950 against Tibet and UN forces in Korea, in 1962 against India, in 1969 against the Soviet Union, in 1974 against South Vietnam, and in 1979 against Vietnam. For the Chinese, *shi* in this context may be thought of as a "stratagem" intended to be a masterstroke, not just solid but brilliant.[42]

In the Chinese strategic tradition, the greatest hero is Zhuge Liang of the Three Kingdoms, a leader best known for his ingenious and deceptive stratagems. Without question, Chinese science and technology have advanced, and this has emboldened the already powerful cultural conviction that China can get much more with less because it is far better than its adversaries, not only intellectually but also materially.

Such a concept is extremely dangerous, and many conflicts in history have been based on such profoundly misguided beliefs, as with the Japanese decision to attack Great Britain, the Netherlands, and the United States in December 1941. The likelihood is high that the Chinese are guided along a similar path by their strategic worldview. They believe that they possess superior strategic knowledge and ability and that they will always be able to outfox and outmaneuver their foes. Likewise, they have the belief that strategic deception plays a key role in their superior abilities. Within the Han-centric perspective, the Chinese are more cunning and virtuous than the rest. The United States, in contrast, is easily manipulated, although strong and violent just like an adolescent. Naturally, such an approach seriously underestimates the ability of the United States and other countries to identify and respond. The conceit among the Chinese that they can manipulate others is supremely dangerous for the stability of Asia, with potential flash points being the South China or East China Sea disputes and U.S. military involvement in the region.[43]

Throughout history, states have made appeals based on ethnocentrism for purposes of unity, identity, and popular support.[44] This is not social imperialism, generating an enemy by overcoming social or class divisions within a state, as was the case in Wilhelmine Germany. Instead, this is the interaction between the Chinese government and its people. The government educates the people to be proud of China and of being Han. As a result, large segments of the Chinese population are fiercely patriotic as well as ethnocentric and xenophobic. The government may change, but popular sentiments will not, because they are anchored in a core Chinese identity, which is not often questioned within the society.

This unity provides three major advantages. First, it allows the Chinese to have a sense of belonging together, that is to say, a strong collective memory. A fundamental human need is to know where one stands in a community and to which groups one belongs. Han-centric identity answers those questions satisfactorily for most people. Despite their differences, they are one, and they are told so, generation after generation, by their family, culture, history, and government.

Second, it allows the Chinese to have a strong sense of identity, which in turn permits them to weather adversity, secure and confident that the rest of the nation is with them. Knowing that one is not alone but is backed by more than a billion others who share the same thoughts, cultural references, and attitudes is reassuring for each Han Chinese. In truth, they are a society with considerable social capital, which Robert Putnam identifies as central to the prosperity of a community.[45] This makes it far more likely that they will respond to government entreaties to support the nation as it advances or when it is challenged by social or economic problems or by other states.

Third, China is not plagued by self-doubt or guilt about its past. It does not revel in its defeats; instead, it recasts them in a patriotic light, as with the 1979 invasion of Vietnam or abuses of its minorities. China's victories are lauded, and a self-congratulatory image is portrayed. China does not face a significant "culture war" in this regard. This gives the government a considerable advantage as a de facto unicultural state. In sum, it will be hard to cause a loss of confidence with the Chinese.

Chinese Appeals to Racial Solidarity

The Chinese will advance entreaties to the Global South based on "racial solidarity," that is, the need for nonwhite peoples to unite against western imperialism and racism. From the Chinese perspective, the West has exploited Asians since the Portuguese and Dutch arrived in the sixteenth and seventeenth centuries. The Chinese have a natural affinity as victims of white racism. This claim is often made in the context of Sino-Afro relations, where the Chinese have used appeals based on victimhood to advance their interests. For example, Sandra Gillespie argues that racial solidarity was a central theme in Mao's pronouncements on anticolonial and revolutionary movements in Africa and served as justification for the Chinese government's African aid projects, with the Red Guard often rallying support for African causes. Moreover, as Gillespie notes, "Few would have dared to openly express hostility to people from the Third World."[46]

The history of the Cold War is rife with efforts by the Chinese to cast or define themselves as separate from the West and from the Soviet Union. The Cuban Missile Crisis occurred during the height of the Sino-Soviet split, and the Chinese wasted no time lambasting the Soviets for their behavior during the crisis and their negotiated compromise that brought the crisis to its end. Most important, the Chinese made appeals to the Cubans at this time, some of which were based on racist appeals. Reflecting on China's actions, Nikita Khrushchev recounted in his memoirs: "The Chinese were making a lot of noise publicly, as well as buzzing in Castro's ear, 'Just remember, you can't trust the imperialists to keep any promises they make!' In other words, the Chinese exploited the episode to discredit us in the eyes of the Cubans."[47]

Racial solidarity is easy for the Chinese to accomplish. They can frame international politics in terms of a "racial balance of power" and cast appeals to the Global South along the lines of "now is the time for nonwhites to dominate international politics." Such pleas immediately bring to mind the propaganda of the Japanese "Greater East Asian Co-Prosperity Sphere" during Tokyo's invasion of China, and later in World War II, when the slogan "Asia for the Asians" was popular.

As is increasingly demonstrated, these entreaties meet with only mixed success at best due to Chinese business practices, racism, and a condescending attitude toward Africans in the belief that they need Chinese leadership.[48] According to Shanshan Lan, since the late 1990s China has revived the Maoist discourse "of Sino-African solidarity and narrated the current China/African relations as 'a continuation of an old friendship' that is based in Mao's anti-colonial and anti-racist agenda."[49] In 2005, the Chinese media touted the fiftieth anniversary of the Bandung Conference and the "Bandung Spirit" of "South-South" cooperation, and the government of China proclaimed the year 2006 to be "the Year of Africa," while both the government and media emphasized shared Sino-African experiences of colonialism and racial discrimination. Despite these messages, as Vera Fennell notes, the CCP "may have control over the message about race, but it may have increasingly less control over those individuals and companies that represent China in Africa."[50]

The West should not underestimate how appealing this message will be to many in the Global South. This is because China's wealth can make it an attractive partner for actors willing to discount or dismiss Chinese biases. For example, as Deborah Brautigam relates, "It is not difficult to get African government officials to expound on the contrast between China's approach and the detailed and intrusive conditions often considered necessary by international donors. . . . As the former Sierra Leone government minister Dr. Sesay told me, the Chinese will simply build a school, a hospital, and then supply a team of doctors to run it. . . .

The World Bank will say: 'You must not have so many teachers on your payroll. You must employ some expatriate staff. You must cut down on your wages.' The Chinese will not do this. They will not say, 'You must do this, do that, do this!'"[51]

In addition, the United States should fully anticipate that as Chinese power grows, so too will its status as an icon of Asian solidarity and triumph as well as the solidarity and triumph of the Global South. So this iconic status will serve as a mechanism of Chinese diplomacy, ideology, and soft power.

Han-Centrism Hinders Relations with the Global South

Han nationalism makes it difficult for China to advance a positive message in Africa, Latin America, and the Middle East. The Han-centric worldview offers a hierarchy of looking at other groups—darker skin is lower class, and race matters—and emphasizes racial stereotypes that portray certain ethnic groups as backward, dirty, and predisposed to violent crime.

In particular, Chinese business practices in Africa appear to be shaped by Han-centrism. There are many accounts now of the explicit racism of Chinese managers working in Africa.[52] They want to appeal to the Third World on a racial basis, but their bigotry often defeats what otherwise might be an attractive message. As a result, these offers fall on deaf ears.

The Chinese Communist Party is very good at promoting economic growth. If the economy declines, it will affect the Party's legitimacy. Therefore, unemployment is a central concern of the Party—and with good reason, since there are 25 million new people to employ each year, and so the economy must support employment.[53] To safeguard against unemployment, and in a classic case of imperialism straight out of Vladimir Lenin's *Imperialism: The Highest Stage of Capitalism*, the Chinese are dumping goods into Africa and undermining African businesses. The consequences for Africa are considerable.

China's approach often meets resistance due to its own ham-fisted grab for the resources it needs at the cost of local communities. Africans increasingly see China as a "New Colonialist."[54] Large numbers of Chinese are settling in Africa, where typically they employ other Chinese and not Africans, purchase raw material for processing elsewhere, and sell to foreign markets in the classic fashion of European imperialism that occurred more than a century ago.

As Guy Scott, former agricultural minister, member of the Zambian parliament, and former head of the Patriotic Front Party, said: "If you go to a market you find Chinese selling beansprouts and cabbages. What is the point of letting them do that? There's a lot of Chinese doing construction. Zambians can do that. The Chinese building firms are undercutting Zambian firms. . . . Our textile factories can't compete with cheap Chinese imports subsidized by a foreign government. People are saying, 'We've had bad people before. The whites were bad, the Indians were worse, but the Chinese are the worst of all.'"[55]

Dipak Patel, former Zambian minister of trade and industry, commented that the Zambian government had to be clear "what type of investment it wants. If it is just shipping out resources and shipping in cheap goods and people, that's not to our benefit. We in Zambia need to be very careful of this new scramble for Africa. What's happening is that the Chinese are very aggressive. They have a strategic plan."[56]

In Africa, the Chinese have been difficult trading partners. Local traders are angry about the influx and business practices of small-scale Chinese traders in Nairobi, Kenya, and they have circulated anti-Chinese leaflets and staged street protests. On August 20, 2012, Mwaura Samora wrote in the Kenyan *Daily Nation*, "As you read this, Chinese archaeologists are digging up Malindi, where they hope to unearth evidence of their presence in the East African coast dating way back to the Ming Dynasty, when Chinese admiral Zheng He is said to have rounded the coast of Somalia and sailed down to the Mozambique Channel. The

Ming Dynasty was in power from 1368 to 1644. . . . Well, centuries after the Ming Dynasty, when sailors blazed the trail, Chinese corporations are here, almost ubiquitously, building roads and skyscrapers. And with them have come small-scale traders . . . and a source of friction."[57]

The article continues: "They are a crafty lot," said a Luthuli Avenue–based generator and public address system dealer who identified himself as Karis. The Chinese come "disguised as customers and ask for our prices, only to go back to their country and bring to the market the same products at a much lower price." According to Karis, the Chinese employ Kenyan salesmen only to offload them after building a client base and learning local business dynamics. Another said: "Most don't pay rent or city council levies. They are eating into our client base." Protesters said that "Kenya's government should enforce taxes on Chinese imports and traders and conduct studies on why they can sell goods cheaper than local traders. A statement from China's embassy in Nairobi noted its efforts to educate Chinese companies and citizens in Kenya to operate businesses within the law and live together in harmony with the local people." The embassy expressed concern over leaflets that "threaten both the Chinese business people in Kenya and the Kenyan people."[58]

Nairobi is not the only African city swarming with the enterprising merchants from China. Small-scale traders in Dakar, Lusaka, Luanda, Maputo, and elsewhere are contending with the entry of the dragon. As Samora reported, the government of Malawi passed a law in August 2012 to protect local vendors by confining foreign traders to the country's four major cities (Lilongwe, Blantyre, Mzuzu, and Zomba) and requiring them to deposit $250,000 in the country's central bank. "The new law clearly outlines what kind of businesses foreign investors will be allowed to get involved in." Samora quoted Malawi's minister of trade, John Bande, as saying: "We will not accept foreigners to come all the way from China and open small businesses and shops in the rural areas of this country and compete with local traders."[59]

A documentary by Kenya's A24 Media, *Chinese Fuel Resurgence in Ivory Poaching*, claimed that 50 percent of poaching incidents in Kenya today happen within a twenty-mile radius from Chinese road-building projects. Major poaching activities were reported in areas such as Tsavo and Amboseli where the Chinese were grading or constructing roads. "I think there is a link between the number of Chinese who have come into Africa recently and elephant ivory purchasing," explained Dr. Esmond Bradley-Martin, a conservationist interviewed in the documentary. "For instance, in about 2000/2001, there was something like 75,000 Chinese working in Africa. Now the figure is well over 500,000, and the Chinese are being caught all over Africa. . . . In Kenya they have been caught with ivory coming in from Congo and Cameroon."[60]

Energy resources are the major economic reason for China's expanding presence in Africa.[61] Although about one-third of China's oil imports come from Angola, Sudan, Congo, Equatorial Guinea, Chad, and Nigeria, making China the third largest trading partner of Africa after the United States and France, many of China's actions raise suspicions among Africans that Beijing's approach to the continent is guided only by a concept of expedient looting of resources. To advance that aim, any regime or politician, however loathsome, will be supported or dropped abruptly if circumstances change. This widespread conviction is making Africans into something far different from the rather eager, ideologically committed, and politically compliant partners of the 1960s. At the same time, China's approach to Africa is undermining its often-reiterated positions of noninterference in foreign states, equality, respect, and so on, not only in Africa but worldwide, where Beijing is increasingly seen as an unscrupulous player.[62]

The impact of energy resources and prices may make it difficult for China to follow the same path to development, propelled by cheap energy, that lifted the states of Europe and North America. This profound fact is inescapable, no matter how much oil the Chinese acquire in Latin America or Africa. Moreover, the oil that China imports contains considerable risk. Oil is transported around the world in a fleet of about four thousand tankers, many of which serve the needs of multiple customers. That procession could easily be closed by attack or blockade of the sources, such as with Saudi Arabia. To the west, in the Red Sea, is a single set of Saudi loading facilities, but the Red Sea, too, is easily blocked. China has loading facilities and a military base in Djibouti on the Red Sea and a strong presence, including peacekeepers, in South Sudan.[63] Although a serious adversary could sabotage this connection with little difficulty, it is evidence of China's expanding activities in Africa—developments that are far harder to stop. It is in sum the abandonment of Beijing's long-held policy of not interfering.

In addition, the path to China is an obstacle course of maritime choke points. The entrance to the Straits of Malacca is controlled by the Indian Andaman and Nicobar Islands, which provide the Indians with considerable leverage in a potential conflict with China. The Straits are between Malaysia and Indonesia, Muslim countries deeply suspicious of their Chinese minorities. At the Philip Channel, the easternmost part of the Strait passing Singapore, the waterway is at least a mile wide. Given these obstacles, it is questionable whether dependence on significant petroleum imports is viable for China. To combat this, the Chinese are building ports in Pakistan and Myanmar, and the Belt and Road Initiative will offset that vulnerability to some degree by strengthening reliable lines of communication to Central and Southwest Asia and Europe.

Chinese business practices are a little different in Latin America. Chinese companies want to increase their investments in Latin America and expand beyond the focus on mining and resources. They are moving increasingly into supermarkets, which will help China avoid resistance to its further expansion.[64] In Africa especially, China has been criticized for channeling much of its investment into natural-resource extraction, for importing Chinese labor on infrastructure construction projects, and for swamping local markets with cheap goods. The concern now is that a similar pattern could emerge in Latin America. China pushes for "what it wants, but Latin America doesn't think the same," said Wu Guoping, assistant director of the Institute of Latin American Studies, Chinese Academy of Social Sciences, at a September 2012 conference on Chinese investment in Latin America. Warning that trade and investment between China and Latin America was not "complementary" and entailed risks, he added, "China has to look for a new strategy for Latin America."[65]

Chinese foreign investment in Latin America has surged, and that investment, plus increasingly active lending, has given China greater sway in an area long considered a bulwark of U.S. influence. However, China is looking for new markets to manufacture and sell more sophisticated products, such as cars and power-generation equipment. It could also help avoid tensions such as those with African countries—a subject of discussion during a visit by African leaders to Beijing in July 2012. During a trip to Latin America in June, Chinese premier Wen Jiabao proposed a $5 billion cooperation fund for infrastructure investment and a $10 billion credit line to support the construction and infrastructure industries in the region.

Nonetheless, not everyone in the area embraces investment by Chinese companies. There is growing concern about corruption and Chinese business practices.[66] Argentina and Brazil have prohibited land sales to the Chinese, leading the way for other Latin American states. Brazilian manufacturers are especially concerned by the prospect of a more active China in the region. The Brazilian government has become aware that China is enriching raw materials exporters while weakening its industry. The result has been a call for tariff barriers against the Chinese. According to eminent Sinologist June Teufel Dreyer: "Chinese-made shoes are cutting into the shoe industry there and Chinese cars have the potential to bankrupt locally made ones. Still, it's a matter of whose ox is being gored. Many sellers of raw materials are very happy to have the Chinese market."[67] As Asim al-Moghrabi, Sudan's leading environmental expert on the Nile River, said of Chinese support for a dam on that river: "The

Chinese are fast and cheap, and to top it all they give you loans. How were we supposed to say no?"[68]

Spanish journalists Juan Pablo Cardenal and Heriberto Araújo have long studied the business practices of "China, Inc." in the world and have distilled the essence of what makes China such a successful and attractive partner: "The formula 'your resources for my loans and/or infrastructure' is common between China and its partner countries, who are always rich in natural resources. Few nations in the so-called 'developing world' can resist being seduced by China's vast supplies of quick and easy money. . . . The temptation to secure millions of dollars in loans—often at preferential rates—in return for providing China with long-term acquiescence to exploit their natural resources is generally far too strong."[69]

Yet it is not just a marriage of supply and demand. What makes the Chinese so competitive is "China's effective use of all the cogs in the state's machinery in order to secure juicy contracts and strategic investments in countries that are in dire need of funding. The financial (banks), economic (state-owned companies), and political institutions . . . work together as one body to achieve the country's national objectives." As a result, they say, the "leitmotif is always the same: obtaining or guaranteeing China's long-term supply of natural resources, ousting the competition, and gaining in terms of political influence and power."[70]

This also provides insight into why Chinese corporations frequently act with little regard for the negative externalities that their business practices impose on the economy and environment. The lack of a "civil society, a free press or rule of law to keep watch, set limits, and denounce or punish the inappropriate actions of China's corporations abroad" means that it can only be done in the countries themselves or through international pressure.[71] Deleterious Chinese business practices often result in an economy and business culture in which there are few checks and balances.

5 Han-Centrism Provides Strategic Asymmetries for the United States

When two emperors appear simultaneously, one must be destroyed.
—Han dynasty emperor Wen-Di, second century AD

This chapter evaluates China's soft power means to advance its interests—its ability to provide aid, infrastructure with "few strings attached," and foreign investment with little political interference within the country or objections due to regime type. The international stage is set for the struggle between Beijing's model for development and international politics, capitalism wedded to authoritarianism, versus Washington's capitalism wedded to political freedom.

Despite significant Chinese advantages, we also address measures that the United States may advance to take strategic advantage of Han-centrism. To further this goal, the chapter will consider each mechanism in turn, beginning with the positive image the United States may adopt in the competition for ideas in international politics. Han-centrism is a major strategic asymmetry, areas of comparative advantage in a competitive relationship, for the United States.[1] We discuss five major implications for the United States and other western states. Each of these implications provides a foundation for messages designed to highlight the implications of Han-centrism. The illumination of the consequences of Han-centrism provides the opportunity to undermine or weaken China's position in the world.

In our current dealings with China, there are many lessons to be learned from the Cold War. Using history as our guide, we should expect that there will also be a struggle in the realm of ideas for the support and loyalty of allies throughout the world.

The Cold War contained a stark and fierce global struggle over ideology and ideas: Was capitalism or communism the superior economic system? What about representative democracy or totalitarianism? Was human freedom to be valued over the belief in the inevitability of socialism? The present period concerns equally weighty issues. This global struggle over ideas receives scant attention in the West. Indeed, sensitivity to the existence of the struggle and concern over its outcome gather little traction even in the specialized national security press and think tanks. However, as with many asymmetries, the lack of attention does not equal an absence of significance.

China's Soft Power Advantages and the Beijing Consensus

A large part of the competition between the United States and China occurs in the realm of "soft power." The term was conceived in 1990 by Joseph S. Nye Jr., who argued that the United States had large reserves of power and influence that were separate from its "hard power," or traditional economic, diplomatic, and military means of advancing its interests. In contrast, soft power is about "getting others to want what you want" or "the ability to shape the preferences of others . . . getting what you want through attraction rather than coercion or payments. It arises from the attractiveness of a country's culture, political ideals, and policies. When our policies are seen as legitimate in the eyes of others, our soft power is enhanced."[2]

More generally, the components of soft power are also language and the willingness or desire of other peoples to learn the dominant language, whether that is English or Mandarin, overseas investments, development assistance, cultural influence, film, television, other aspects of popular culture, education, travel, tourism, or disaster relief.

One of China's most important soft power assets is their informal policy of "no strings" attached to the aid provided to governments in developing countries. The recipient governments of PRC trade and investment money are often authoritarian and so are attracted to the fact that Chinese aid comes without human rights conditions, good governance requirements, or environmental quality regulations that typically accompany western funding. China markets itself as being more efficient and less intrusive for its recipients and perceives this as a key competitive advantage over the West when wooing governments.

By all accounts, it works. According to Senegal president Abdoulaye Wade, "I have found that a contract that would take five years to discuss, negotiate, and sign with the World Bank takes three months when we deal with Chinese authorities. I am a firm believer in good governance and the rule of law. But when bureaucracy and senseless red tape impede our ability to act—and when poverty persists while international functionaries drag their feet—African leaders have an obligation to opt for swifter solutions."[3]

While the West may be able to reduce red tape to some degree, there is no desire or willingness at this stage to match Beijing's flexibility and unrestricted investments while holding the recipients of its aid to no international standards. Accordingly, the West should expect its influence to wane to the degree that influence is determined by aid.

A second soft power advantage Beijing has is the fact that much of its foreign investment is carried out by its strong state-owned sector. These state corporations lack transparency, have considerable wealth supported by the government, and operate without constraints such as annual public reporting. Unlike most western corporations, which lack government patronage and must answer to their shareholders, Chinese state-owned companies have the luxury of being able to take a long-term strategic view that advances Chinese national priorities without having to be concerned about immediate profits, unlike western firms.

In the competition with China, its rapid rise is a growing source of international influence, investment, and political and economic power. For many observers, China is seen as trying to project soft power by portraying its own system as an alternative model of economic development.[4] In addition, through Confucian institutes and other sources, China is advancing its language, history, and civilization as an alternative to the United States and the West.[5]

When we consider its history, it is clear that the ideological struggle with China has been a long one. The Cold War served as the venue for fierce ideational conflict between Beijing and Washington. With the warming of relations in the 1970s and 1980s, this conflict cooled, only to commence again after the Cold War's end. China analyst Steven Mosher has studied the ups and downs of the United States' periods of strong support and hatred for China.[6]

The first round of this struggle took place two decades ago in the context of the Asian Values school of thought advanced by Lee Kuan Yew in contrast to Francis Fukuyama's "End of History" thesis—the triumph of western ideas concerning capitalism and liberal democratic government.[7] This debate has not gone away but has segued into the struggle over rival economic systems, the "Washington Consensus" versus the "Beijing Consensus."

Does the Washington Consensus solution to modernization—the belief in freedom, free markets, and the rule of law—triumph over the Beijing Consensus model, which advances authoritarian government, state-led economic development, protected markets, and acceptable corruption and crony capitalism? Empirically the Beijing Consensus has gained traction with countries that now seek to follow China's path to economic development.[8]

The advantages China receives from engaging in this ideological-cum-economic-cum-strategic struggle are significant. China undermines U.S. power and western economic institutions and helps to create the conditions to replace them with alternatives preferred by China, such as the Asian Infrastructure Investment Bank (AIIB, the first Asian-based international bank to be independent of western institutions) and the Belt and Road Initiative (BRI), formerly called the One Belt One Road (OBOR) Initiative, which envisions investing more than $124 billion to build a land corridor from China to Europe based on railroads and highways.[9] Of course, OBOR takes its inspiration from the ancient Silk Road, which ran from China to Europe via central Asia. The land corridor, the "Silk Road Economic Belt," will be twinned with a sea corridor, the "Twenty-First Century Maritime Silk Road," through Southeast Asia, the Indian Ocean, to the Mediterranean, and will include modernized ports in Asia, Africa, Europe, and the Middle East. The land and sea corridors will ensure that China is tied to markets across the Eurasian continents and can be supplied with energy and other resources from multiple sources, which greatly complicates any attempt to interdict China's lines of communication.[10] China has set a goal of $2.5 trillion in trade with OBOR countries by 2025.[11] Often overlooked in Xi's announcement and subsequent statements was a vague description that all trade within the region would be handled through intraregional local currency convertibility, that is, a new currency to replace the dollar and thus weaken U.S. influence.[12]

These institutions will advance Chinese interests in contrast to American-dominated institutions such as the World Bank, International Monetary Fund, and, with Japan, the Asian Development Bank. Equally important, the creation of the AIIB indicates that China is downgrading its aims for the New Development Bank, which was founded with Brazil, Russia, and India in 2014. If realized, China's initiatives would encompass 4.4 billion people, 64 countries, and a combined economic output of $21 trillion—roughly twice the annual gross domestic product of China.

According to Xue Li, the director of the International Strategy Research Office of the World Politics and Economics Research Institute of the Chinese Academy of Social Sciences, the leading official think tank in China, the "One Belt One Road is an attempt and a pathway for China to change from being a regional power with worldwide influence to a world power with comprehensive power." Indeed, Xue calls it "China's Marshall Plan."[13] However, the Marshall Plan is a poor comparison, as it accelerated European recovery after a devastating war. In contrast, China's diplomacy uses economic carrots to ensure dominant influence in these states that might have weak infrastructure but are not in urgent need of aid to feed, clothe, and house their people, as were European states after World War II.

The second advantage for China in this ideological struggle is that China's success is evidenced by its rising economic and military power, in contrast to the United States' relative decline. This is an important perception in the minds of many leaders and other audiences in global politics. If the perception is that the United States is in decline, it would be wise to back the new dominant state rather than to be linked to the weakened power.

Another advantage is that it assists with alliance relationships by giving developing countries and emerging markets the freedom to reject western conditions of financial engagement. For example, China also provides states in economic crisis, such as Angola, Cambodia, Chad, Iran, Myanmar, Sudan, Venezuela, and Uzbekistan, with an alternative to following the dictates of western institutions like the International Monetary Fund. Also, they no longer must choose between emulating the western model or rejecting capitalism. With China, these states have a nonwestern capitalistic model to follow, which promises growth while maintaining authoritarian government.

Beijing recognizes what Washington did in the 1940s: when it comes to alliances, birds of a feather flock together. The hegemon creates the alliance structure by enticing or imposing similar economic systems or economic interests and similar ideologies to generate and sustain alliances. The similarity may come from a negative component, unification caused by opposition to Washington, or from a positive element, accepting and welcoming Beijing's organizing principles and political beliefs, governmental structure, or economic operation. It is the latter, of course, that is better for the health and longevity of the alliance. The new elite of the country accepts the values, principles, and norms of Washington's order, and it does so generation after generation.

Indeed, one of the great open secrets of Washington's success in creating an international order consistent with its interests was that it required the political, economic, legal, and cultural elite of West Germany, Italy, and Japan to conform to its major values.[14] To be sure, the process was resisted in some quarters—we can recall the anti-Americanism of High Tories like Harold Macmillan and Anthony Eden—but opposition was to no avail. Leaders could be replaced if they strayed too far from Washington's objectives. Even France under Charles de Gaulle, a thorn in Washington's side if ever there was one, maintained dovetailed strategic interests in Europe once it was clear that West German chancellor Konrad Adenauer would not join him in a "Third Way," an alliance to balance the Soviet Union and the United States.

Today China's model seems to be more attractive than any "Third Way" of the Cold War. Stefan Halper argues that China's model is more appealing to the developing world and middle-sized powers, like Iran, Indonesia, Nigeria, Turkey, and Vietnam, than America's market-democratic model captured in the Washington Consensus.[15] China's model gives rise to a strategic challenge for the United States, accelerates the "power shift" from the United States to China, and raises the possibility that the world will be increasingly unsympathetic to the democratic principles and values of the West and to U.S. leadership.

Indeed, China is pushing hard in this direction. U.S. decision makers must recognize the alternative message China is developing. Like the

Soviets, they seek to cloak their rise using attractive rhetoric, appeals to reason, and a desire for peace. The appeal is to a "peaceful growth," a "moral standing," and Confucianism, rather than the Soviet Union's "march of history," but the ideational threat is even greater than the significant threat posed by the Soviet Union. An excellent example is Yan Xuetong's [阎学通] telling book on ancient Chinese political thought and how it informs the rise of China today.[16] His essential argument is that a stable international order stems from the leadership of a humane authority that has strong "moral standing" and whose rule is accepted rather than hegemonic with an emphasis on hard power.

It is an important argument because of what it reveals. First, China sees its rise to dominance as the manifestation of rule by "humane authority." This is nothing new. It is a rule of international politics that rising hegemons—from Rome's desire to share the benefits and glory of its empire with its conquered peoples, to France's *mission civilisatrice*, to Russia's "Near Abroad"—perceive themselves to be acting for a greater good and are nonplussed when they encounter any opposition to their obviously beneficial rule. Second, China perceives the United States as unable to achieve such a lofty goal when it was the dominant state, but it is an obligation of the Chinese to provide a "better model for society" and international order than that provided by the United States. Third, China will return to its traditional policy of "Sinification," requiring weaker states to recognize Chinese leadership and adapt to what Beijing wishes under the mantle of "wise" or "humane" direction.

Five Major Implications for the United States

A major strategic objective for the United States is to counter Chinese soft power. While this is a formidable task, the United States has many advantages. These combine to yield powerful asymmetries for the United States. First, while it is beyond the boundaries of this study, it must be noted that an important exception to this increasing acceptance of the

Beijing Consensus is India. India's great strengths are that it is democratic and that it embraces, in its own way, private enterprise. Like the United States, New Delhi has a commitment to entrepreneurship as the source of innovation and growth. This provides the United States with a continued stake in India's economic growth and prosperity for obvious commercial reasons and global economic expansion, but also for strategic reasons and as an alternative to the Beijing Consensus.[17]

Second, and directly relevant to this study, the United States must recognize that it still retains a dominant image in the world. It has an open society, economy, universal ideology that protects individual liberty and freedom, a history of humanitarian aid, an absence of territorial disputes, and no desire to dominate. Moreover, it has a significant advantage in the fact that it is not a strongly nationalist state and China is.

Han-Centrism Is the Source of China's Hegemonic Behavior

Naturally enough, one of the key insights into Chinese future behavior is its past. Analysts do have insight into how China will behave in the future based on its identity and self-perception in the past when it was the hegemon of Asia—the known world as far as China was concerned.[18] As the study has shown, when Han-centrism triumphs, China sees itself as the center of the universe, while all others are inferior. That is not an attractive model for gaining allies.

Chinese ethnocentrism, xenophobia, and even racism will surface inevitably in their dealings with the rest of the world. As they become more powerful, they will be less restrained about evincing these behaviors and alienating people. No doubt Chinese money and power can buy allies of a kind and for a period of time, but they are likely to be more fragile than the alliance relationships forged by the United States through its seventy years of engagement.

This study concurs with Martin Jacques's statement: "For perhaps the next half-century, it seems unlikely that China will be particularly aggressive. History will continue to weigh very heavily on how it handles its growing power, counselling caution and restraint. On the other hand, as China becomes more self-confident, a millennia-old sense of superiority will be increasingly evident in Chinese attitudes. But rather than being imperialistic in the traditional Western sense—though this will, over time, become a growing feature as it acquires the interests and instincts of a superpower—China will be characterized by a strongly hierarchical view of the world, embodying the belief that it represents a higher form of civilization than any other."[19]

This recognition dovetails with historian Wang Gungwu's [王赓武] argument that the tributary system was based on hierarchical principles, the most important of which "is the principle of superiority."[20] This combination of hierarchy and superiority will reveal itself in China's relations with the rest of the world. One suspects that it will do so first, and most clearly, in China's attitude toward Africa and Southeast Asia. Both are barometers of Chinese behavior, and what we are witnessing is that China is acting boldly, in accord with the principles of power politics and economic exploitation. This is directly opposed to any "Confucian" or benign foreign policy.

Wang suggests that even when China was forced to abandon the tributary system and adapt to the humiliations and disciplines of the Westphalian system, in which all states are sovereign and enjoy formal equality, China never accepted it. "This doubt partly explains the current fear that, when given the chance, the Chinese may wish to go back to their long-hallowed tradition of treating foreign countries as all alike but equal and inferior to China."[21]

The size of its population, profundity of its culture, and the longevity of its civilization mean that China will always have a different attitude toward its place in the world from the European states and the United States. China has always believed itself to be universal, having what Jacques calls the "Middle Kingdom mentality."[22] In a very real sense,

China does not desire to run the world, because it already believes itself to be the center of the world, which is its natural role and position. As it becomes a superpower, this attitude will strengthen. In consequence, China will probably be less aggressive than the imperialist powers of the West, but that does not mean that it will not resort to force or that it will be less assertive or less determined to impose its will. Indeed, U.S. decision makers should expect that it will do so. Yet it will be guided by the inherent belief in its own superiority and the "proper" hierarchy of relations, of which China is the center.

What William Faulkner wrote of life in the American South in his novel *Requiem for a Nun* is true of China today: "The past is never dead. It isn't even past." Like almost all states, China's past informs its view of international politics. But China is a civilizational state, and so it will be back to the future, once China is powerful enough. If China is successful, the world is likely to witness a return to some form of the tribute model of international politics and international leadership, the *koutou*.

Inklings of what this modern form of the tributary system might entail were witnessed at the May 2017 unveiling of the latest version of the Belt and Road Initiative. Particularly relevant were the remarks of the Italian and Greek prime ministers, both states heavily in debt and looking to China as a source of relief. In Beijing, Italian prime minister Paolo Gentiloni stated that "Italy can be a protagonist in this grand scheme that China so much values. . . . This is a great opportunity for us, and my presence here underscores how important it is to us." Greek prime minister Alexis Tsipras emphasized China's role as an investor in the ports of Piraeus near Athens and Soufli in the Evros region, remarking that the two ports are symbols of Sino-Greek cooperation. Piraeus, for reasons that might be appreciated by Xi, is called the "head of the dragon" in Europe, a terminus of the BRI. The second port is called Soufli for reasons that might be less appreciated by Xi: "because it was 'the first European ground touched by the two monks who centuries ago travelled on the Silk Road and brought to Europe the first silkworm eggs hidden in their canes,' a reference to the famous episode of the two Byzantine monks who smuggled silkworm eggs from China during the reign of Justinian I," which permitted the Byzantines to develop their own silk industry and break China's monopoly.[23]

The comments and actions of these European leaders might be considered simply diplomatic and politic statements from those seeking to benefit from BRI. But from the Chinese perspective, it is a symbol of China's return to pride of place in global politics, with world leaders in awe of Chinese accomplishments and tacitly paying tribute to China's great project and, more significantly, leadership and power. As Liu Mingfu explained, "In East Asia's tribute system, China was the superior state, and many of its neighbouring states were vassal states, and they maintained a relationship of tribute and rewards. This was a special regional system through which they maintained friendly relations and provided mutual aid. The appeal and influence of ancient China's political, economic, and cultural advantages were such that smaller neighbouring states naturally fell into orbit around China."[24]

However, despite the felicitous words of the prime ministers of European debtor states, or the positive and benign description by Liu, the *koutou* is not an attractive model. In Chinese history, foreign political entities often had to accept it. Today international politics has changed significantly since the dominance of the koutou before 1839. There are other sources and centers of power for states wishing to avoid the koutou, including maintaining an alliance with the United States. Concern that China harbors a hierarchical view of its relations with weaker states yields a significant asymmetry for the United States. The koutou provides empirical evidence of how the Chinese see other states and other peoples.

Accordingly, U.S. decision makers may tailor messages to the international community to aid its alliances among those allies that might be weakening in support, to augment its soft power, and to weaken the attractiveness of the Beijing Consensus and China as a model for the world. We suggest the following themes that the United States and other states might draw upon as asymmetrical messages to weaken China's support in the world. The first should be to advance a "reality check" to the global community: "how do Chinese words match Chinese deeds when it comes to treating people fairly and equally?"

The second theme is to introduce fault: "why has the Chinese government done so little to hinder the xenophobia, chauvinism, and racism of Han nationalism? Rather, the CCP often supports this Han-centric worldview, which portrays the non-Han, be it the Uighur in Xinjiang or Africans working for Chinese firms, as backward and inferior. Attention needs to be called to how Han-centrism encourages exploitative business practices overseas and the continued mistreatment of ethnic minorities within Chinese society.

A third theme is to suggest that there is something profoundly wrong with this worldview: "why are the Chinese unable to change their Han-centric views?" Or that there is something deeply iniquitous with modern Chinese society or something fundamentally wrong with their political elite: "why is China an exclusionary state—a closed society, with severe limits on immigration and human rights?"

Furthermore, "why does the Chinese government support eugenics generations after it has been discredited in the West?" The Chinese are strong supporters of such policies and always have been. The belief in eugenics (*yousheng* [优生]) remains as strong today as it has been in the past and is captured in an ancient Chinese saying: "Sow melons and you will reap melons, plant beans and you will harvest beans" [种瓜得瓜,种豆得豆]. Or, as Confucius says in *The Analects*, "Superior intelligence and inferior stupidity cannot be changed" [唯大智与下愚不移].[25] The international community needs to recognize that, as racist expressions are too frequent in China, so too are eugenicist ideas.

Historically, many countries have had eugenics programs—the United

States, Sweden, France, the UK, and most notoriously, Germany. These policies were advanced to control people, promoting reproduction by some and restraining the freedoms of others. Eugenics provided scientific authority and a solution to social fears, lent respectability to racial prejudice and class bias, and legitimized sterilization policies. Most important, it allowed leaders to portray their societies as an organic body governed by biological laws. In the West, they were ended in the 1960s due to concern over their value and the violation of individual liberties. Thus explicit ties may be drawn by critics of the Chinese government's eugenicist policies to the historical actions and policies of many states in the West, since these states embraced eugenics before rejecting the idea as repugnant. Yet Beijing continues to do so long after it has been discredited.[26]

The PRC passed a law in 1995 aimed at restricting births deemed to be imperfect. It suggests that in order to prevent "inferior births," those "deemed unsuitable for reproduction" should undergo sterilization or abortion or be compelled to remain celibate. China has a wide eugenic campaign aimed at the general public to restrict "imperfect" births. The policies and laws adopted have a strong coercive element to them, which, at its heart, seeks to prevent reproduction by "unfit" people. Twinned with the coercive approach is a pedagogical one, where young people are educated about the need to have a sense of the reproductive responsibility of every citizen.[27]

As the preeminent scholar of race and eugenics in China, Frank Dikötter, writes, "In the name of a more eugenic future, conjugal couples are enjoined strictly to monitor their reproductive behaviour and exercise self-discipline before, during, and after conception. The choice of a partner, the age of marriage, the timing of conception, and even the quality of the semen are all claimed to influence the health of future offspring significantly." To promote this, the government controls the medical knowledge available to prospective parents. The medical knowledge "dispensed in eugenic campaigns is not designed to enable informed individual choices in reproductive matters, but to instill a moral message of sexual restraint and reproductive duty in the name of collective health." In China, eugenics promotes "a biologising vision of society in which the reproductive rights of individuals are subordinated to the rights of an abstract collectivity."[28]

Within China, appeals to "strengthening the race" and improving the state are common in the educational system. Powered by the prestige of science, eugenics allows the Chinese government to advance their policies as objective statements grounded in the laws of evolutionary science. It will be shocking for many in the West to learn that eugenicist ideas are medical policy in China. Common justifications are that the disabled will never be able to live and work independently, will provide endless misfortunes for their families, and will increase the burden on society while lowering the quality of population.

In addition, the costs of maintaining congenitally handicapped people are often invoked to justify eugenic policies. As Chen Muhua, vice president of the Standing Committee of the National People's Congress and president of the Women's Federation, declared in 1991: "Eugenics not only affects the success of the state and the prosperity of the race, but also the well-being of the people and social stability."[29]

Of course, this situation is made worse by China's one-child policy, which places a premium on having the child of the parents' dreams. Abortion, infanticide, especially female infanticide, and foreign adoption are solutions to those who do not.[30] The Party has abandoned its one-child policy, so by 2020 the family itself may decide its size. By 2026 China will return to population increase policies to offset its aging population and anticipated negative economic growth due to its declining population.[31]

Indeed, David Mungello, a historian of religion in China, notes two thousand years of the practice. Its long history, he argues, has several causes, such as a cultural preference for male children, poverty, famine, war, and other natural disasters, and was more prevalent in southern than northern provinces.[32]

It is a major human rights violation that a one-party state controls the expression of dissenting opinion and limits the ability of the Chinese people to make their own reproductive choices, while actively promoting eugenicist beliefs and policies. Frankly, in China there is a war against "imperfect births" and those not deemed worthy of life or of reproducing. Accordingly, it falls to observers of China to call attention to these facts.

These themes allow the United States and other concerned countries to challenge China's projected image of an oppressed victim of racism with actual empirical reality: China is a superpower that tolerates strongly xenophobic, racist, and ethnocentric expressions in the public sphere. It is far from a free and tolerant society.

China Will Make Appeals for Racial Solidarity in the Global South

As they did during the Cold War, the Chinese will advance an appeal for alliances with and support to the Global South based on racial solidarity. This message will indeed find favor. For Beijing, this is a key advantage to be used against the United States.

The United States must be prepared for it and poised to counter. In order to do so effectively, there must be recognition about what has changed since the United States last confronted a peer competitor. First, this is a racially different peer opponent. Accordingly, race will be a subtext of every interaction. The United States has never faced a racially different peer competitor. The closest it did was Japan in World War II, and so race adds a new layer into superpower competition that will have advantages for the United States as well as disadvantages.

Second, what it means to be developed or modern has changed. For the Global South, there is not a single modernity but many. Historically, with the exception of Japan, modernity was exclusively western. Over the last half century, we have witnessed the emergence of additional forms of modernization. These are anchored in some western concepts, like capitalism, but ultimately the states themselves, including India and China, are responsible for their ability to mobilize, build upon, and transform their societies.[33] There is the hybridization of what may be learned from the West and regional neighbors, but also through their own history and culture. Thus the continued modernization of Africa will be different than what it was in the past—a hybrid, not Chinese and not western.

Third, in this competition, the expectation should be that the West will have many lessons to learn. In the face of the growing economic success of East Asian states, the West will be forced to learn from these states and incorporate their insights and characteristics, such as with respect to fiscal discipline, the importance of rigorous education, and living within one's means.[34] The bottom line is that modernity need no longer include Enlightenment principles and a western-style rule of law, an independent judiciary, and representative government. While that is true, it must be acknowledged that the West provides a far better model of achievement for respect for human rights and individual identity. Unfortunately, China's growing support for states in Latin America and Africa, building on their success among the Southeast Asian states, may preclude these values and principles.[35] This is due in part to the fact that China possesses the world's greatest ability to build infrastructure, fund infrastructure projects, and support the trade that the expanded infrastructure makes possible. As Singapore journalist and experienced China observer Toh Han Shih writes: "Although China is not the military top dog, its ability to both build thousands of miles of railway and provide the billions of dollars needed to finance them is a killer combination that gives it geopolitical power far greater than simply trade and financial muscle."[36]

China's growing interest in Latin America and the Caribbean is a relatively recent phenomenon in international politics. Beginning in April

2001, with President Jiang Zemin's thirteen-day tour of Latin America, senior Chinese officials have visited Latin America to court regional governments, while Latin American leaders also have been frequent visitors to Beijing, and these ties have grown only closer under Xi's leadership, especially since his 2014 fourteen-day tour.[37] China's primary interest in the region is to gain access to raw materials and energy resources through increased trade and investment. All three of China's oil firms, Sinopec (China Petroleum and Chemical Corporation), CNOOC (China National Offshore Oil Corporation), and CNPC (China National Petroleum Corporation), have moved into Latin America with alacrity.[38] China's second objective is to offset or replace U.S. power in the region over the longer term, as well as to use its presence in the region to collect intelligence against the United States.[39]

In advancing these objectives, the Chinese have been successful.[40] In 2013 China became the world's biggest trading nation, and much of that trade was with Latin America. Since 2009 China has overtaken the United States as the largest trading partner of Brazil, Latin America's biggest economy. Chinese infrastructure projects have also expanded in Latin America. Chinese dam-building companies are targeting the Latin American market, as prior to 2010 there were two Chinese hydropower projects and just four years later there were twenty-two in Argentina, Belize, Costa Rica, Ecuador, Guyana, Honduras, and Peru. In 2013 Mexico announced a $300 billion transportation and infrastructure investment program to be completed in 2018 in which Chinese companies would have a major share.[41] Strong financial support for Cuba, Ecuador, Panama, and Venezuela creates a degree of financial dependence that harkens back to the 1940s and 1950s and the conditions that gave rise to Argentine economist Raúl Prebisch's dependency theory.[42]

As Toh writes, "China has succeeded in Latin America (including the Caribbean and Central America) where the Soviet Union had failed. China has broken through the Monroe Doctrine to expand its influence among the southern neighbors of the U.S." In fact, "what the Soviet Union failed to do with its nuclear missiles in Cuba, China succeeded with its generous investment, financing, and trade deals in Latin America."[43]

China's relationship with, and aid to, African states has expanded greatly. From the formative period in the 1950s until the late 1970s, China offered African countries aid motivated by political objectives, the spread of Maoism at first in conjunction with the Soviet Union and later as a hostile alternative to it. Much of the aid at that time consisted of infrastructure projects, such as railroads, most notably the famed Tanzania-Zambia (TAZARA) railway of the early 1970s, major buildings, and economic developmental projects. Until the late 1970s, China's engagement in Africa was primarily defined by a shared interest in spreading socialist revolutions and participating in Cold War rivalries with the United States and the Soviet Union.

Since its modernization, China has increasingly pursued bilateral ties defined by wealth creation and other positive economic outcomes rather than ideological considerations. In Africa, China continues to support a variety of modernization projects but also African regimes, as the value of African governments who are supportive of China is important now, just as it was during the Cold War. Indeed, since the 1990s, China's rapid growth has heavily informed its interests in Africa. China has touted its doctrine of political noninterference and respect for state sovereignty that aids it in its dealings with African states. The first of China's interests in Africa has been to secure the continent's resources, especially energy resources.[44] To advance that end, Chinese diplomacy labors to ensure that future Chinese aid and investment continue to be welcomed in Africa. Due to its political history and economic success, the PRC sees itself as a leader of developing countries. Its second objective is to offset or replace U.S. and European power in the region over the longer term, as well as to use its presence in the region to advance its interests.

To achieve this, Beijing is acting with dispatch. As of October 2012,

China had launched thirty-one Confucius institutes and five Confucius classrooms in twenty-six African countries. Between 2010 and 2012, China provided 5,710 government scholarships to African countries. It planned to implement the "African Talent Project," which will recruit and support future African leaders by training 30,000 professionals in different fields and providing 18,000 government scholarships. These efforts are fully in keeping with China's advance into Africa through economic and cultural means in order to increase its influence on the continent. Through 2011, China has been Africa's largest trading partner for the third consecutive year, with the trade volume between the two countries reaching a record $166.3 billion.[45]

As renowned Sinologist Arthur Waldron writes, there is a strategic purpose behind Chinese investments in Africa and, one could assume from his logic, elsewhere in the Global South. Waldron argues that China "is seeking a China-centric community, mostly of small and medium-sized states, that could serve as a counterweight to the emerged or emerging powers of the West, Japan, India, and so forth. The Chinese Communist government is most interested not in the welfare of the Chinese people, but in their own regime's survival. The gradual disappearance of communism worries them deeply."[46]

Waldron continues with his assessment of China's interests in Africa: "China's new interest in Africa would be part of an increasingly visible pattern of seeking to create her own set of economic and political friends. Chinese states have historically been uncomfortable with any but hierarchical foreign relations that they dominate." When we review China's situation in the world, "today's China is not particularly happy with her truly advanced Asian neighbors, such as Japan, Korea, and Taiwan, nor is she naturally congenial with India or Southeast Asia, which are less developed, or for that matter with Europe or the United States." However, "in every case, purely economic considerations would suggest ever-closer cooperation, but as a single-party dictatorship in a world where Pakistan and South Africa and Russia hold elections, China worries about political contagion—not to mention the numerous territorial disputes that poison, for example, relations with India. Taking such considerations into mind, two areas of the world look attractive. One is Latin America, the other is Africa."[47]

Of these, Africa is far more strategically important for China: "In the case of Africa, Beijing has the possibility of winning almost fifty allies many rich in resources, while facing little danger of liberal contagion, and not least being at least seemingly in command of the relationship by virtue of superior education, resources, and technology." Waldron writes: "All of these states vote in the United Nations. Many are deeply embedded and influential in international organizations. Furthermore, from Nigeria to Sudan to Tanzania, they offer what may seem to be strategic political and military positions, on the Atlantic, Red Sea, and the Indian Ocean."[48]

Of course, China's approach often meets resistance due to its own ham-fisted and too naked a grab for the resources it needs at the cost of local communities, with the result that they are alienated from the Chinese. China is increasingly seen as a "New Colonialist" power by states in the Global South. Large numbers of Chinese are settling in Africa, where they employ other Chinese and not Africans, purchase raw material for processing elsewhere, and sell to foreign markets in the classic fashion of European imperialists over a century ago. As Toh submits, "By 2011, there were an estimated one million Chinese in Africa involved in a wide range of activities, including trading, investing, building, labouring, and running micro-businesses," but "various studies and eyewitness accounts have described armies of Chinese workers living in military-style enclosed quarters, served with Chinese food and rarely mixing with locals, while working on the many Chinese-financed infrastructure projects throughout Africa."[49]

The essence of the Chinese message to the Global South is a

straightforward rhetorical query: Have the United States or the Europeans ever treated you as equals? In contrast, the Chinese say they come to your country, pay a fair price for your commodities, and build your infrastructure with no strings attached. According to Barry Sautman and Hairong Yan, experts on China's penetration of Africa, a "positive image of China exists despite the prevalence among the Chinese of racist attitudes, which have been experienced both by Africans in China and Africans working alongside Chinese residents in Africa" mostly due to the legacy of colonialism and Third World solidarity.[50] At the same time, it is clear to Africans that the Chinese presence entails deleterious consequences as well. As African political affairs analyst Roland Marchal writes, "Increasingly, China's role in Africa is contested, not by westerners but Africans. Too often, descriptions of China-African relations assume Africans should be happy to get something from China. It is not the case." According to Anthony Desir, a partner in an African resource consultancy, "The problem for China in Africa is it prefers to cultivate relationships with African leaders who kowtow like deferential courtiers. When the people in these countries feel left out and vote out their disconnected leaders, what will China have?"[51]

The United States needs to counter the expansion of Chinese influence by tying into the messages stated above, but adding the important point that there is no culture of antiracism in China, and so there is little hope for change. Messages may be advanced along the following line: "The West confronted racism and developed a strong culture of antiracism. China has not, nor is it likely to do so."

Second, the United States should argue that Chinese business practices are destructive. As discussed in chapter 4, there often is considerable resentment toward the Chinese due to their ruthless business practices, which undercut and destroy African businesses. China is dumping products, very forcefully and carefully marketing products, which ironically fits Lenin's thesis in his classic work *Imperialism* very well concerning the need of capitalists to exploit the Third World to meet the needs of overproduction.

The combination of the two messages, "China has no culture of anti-racism and their business practices are destructive for the locals," would be most effective in making appeals in Africa, Latin America, and the Caribbean.

Third, it is an obvious point, but it must be made by the international community: China has a problematic record when it comes to race and racial equality. For all of their rhetoric on Africa and their "African brothers," one almost blushes at the positive spin by the Chinese and their supporters in the press because the reality of Chinese Han-centrism intervenes.[52] The cold facts of Chinese Han-centrism and racism triumph paeans to Third World solidarity.

Fourth, the message of the United States should be this: We are better than the Chinese for the long-term political and economic development of Africa and its incorporation into world trade and monetary regimes. Washington will assist you with economic aid to offset what you receive from China. Culturally, socially, and politically, the United States is better, because it treats its citizens equally and it recognizes racial equality, the rights of women and the disabled, and civil rights for all of its citizens.

Han-Centrism Threatens Western Values Including Inclusivity and Equality
China's Han-centrism permits a positive image of the United States to be advanced in direct contrast to China's. When compared with China, it is easy to convey the message to the rest of the world that the United States is open and inclusive, whereas China is not. This is because to do so is completely in accord with the principles of the United States and its history. The United States seeks the best people from around the world and permits them to come to the country so that they may prosper, fulfill themselves, innovate, and participate in the economic growth and continued technological innovation in the United States.

Table 1 captures the important societal differences, both positive and negative, between the United States and China. Naturally, the Chinese government is sure to counter with messages about racism, crime, and unrest in the country even before the billingsgate of the 2016 campaign, profound uncertainty about America's direction and future, negative images of Americans, including laziness, individualism, and lack of honor, filial piety, numerous cases of economic hardship and business failures, and individual hard cases of immigrants, minorities, youths, or other Americans.

This is not a "glass half-empty, glass half-full problem." Both societies have positive and negative elements and should be treated as equals. Such relativism is as misplaced today as it was during the Cold War. On the contrary, the society of the United States is profoundly better than China's, and as such, Beijing's efforts to portray a negative image of Americans can be countered easily.

TABLE 1. Major societal differences between the United States and China

United States is an open, free society	China is a closed, authoritarian society
Growing demographically	Aging population
Welcomes immigration	Hostile to immigration
De facto promotes diversity	De facto promotes uniculturalism
Is transparent and able to reach out to the rest of the world	Does not reach out to the rest of the world
Is declining in relative power	Is rising in relative power
Will have less relative wealth in the future	Will have greater relative wealth in the future
Relatively divided society	Relatively homogeneous society
Strong culture of antiracism	Weak culture of antiracism
Promotes minority rights	Suppresses minority rights

This may be done by identifying a modern-day Horatio Alger "rags to riches" story: the poor immigrant rises to the security and comfort of the middle class, or to wealth, through hard work, determination, and honesty. The United States needs to emphasize success, which is readily done. For example, Steve Jobs was the son of a Syrian immigrant. This makes the United States more attractive for information technology and other skilled immigrants from around the world. The projected image of the United States in this regard matches the empirical reality.

Second, American society is inclusive, not exclusive. The fact that immigrants want to come here is proof that the United States is a favorable destination. This is in direct opposition to China, which receives only a small number of immigrants every year, and by far most of them are from the Chinese diaspora. In 1980, 20,000 foreigners stayed in China for more than six months. By the end of 2011, 600,000 did, principally living in Shanghai and coming mostly from Taiwan and the diaspora. But a modest number came from Vietnam (to Guangxi and Guangdong) and from North Korea (to Manchuria). That there are 600,000 in a country of 1.34 billion, which has a net migration loss of almost 500,000, according to the U.S. Census Bureau, compares unfavorably with the United States, where there may be anywhere from 33 to 38 million out of a population of about 320 million.[53] These data demonstrate the reluctance of the Chinese to support immigration.

The Chinese are more than aware of the need to attract a variety of talents, investors, skilled workers, and what the Chinese call "seagulls," foreign businessmen who work with multinationals around the world. Yet it remains very difficult for a foreigner to receive the equivalent of permanent resident status or citizenship.

In contrast to what is possible in China, the election and reelection of Barack Obama as the first black U.S. president and son of a foreigner sends a powerful message to the rest of the world. Obama's presidency was an epochal event that simply would be impossible in China. Moreover, the United States opens its society, universities, military, and economy to immigrants. It has in place affirmative action policies as a matter of state policy that benefit immigrants from racial minorities and those who are women. In sum, the United States is one of the most transparent societies in the world for immigrants.

This message is low-hanging fruit for the United States, but it needs to be advanced as appropriate in international fora and in diplomacy, Track Two diplomacy, and international media. U.S. decision makers should be cognizant that the ideational struggle between the United States and China is occurring right now. China has the upper hand in this because its advance is coordinated and the United States' response seems to be ad hoc, uncoordinated, and dependent on local media or officials whose attention is occasional and whose interests may not dovetail with those of the United States. Accordingly, countervailing messages along the themes suggested need to be advanced to push back against the Chinese and provoke thought among the governing and intellectual elite of developing countries about the true costs of supporting China.

Han-Centrism and U.S. Alliances

Journalists and other media frequently share a multiracial and multi-cultural vision of their societies. Yet they have not treated the problem of Han-centrism with the attention it deserves, in part for the reasons discussed previously concerning academic and intellectual biases with respect to Chinese and western intellectual concepts of Han-centrism, xenophobia, and racism. To redress this imbalance, scholars may call attention to racism through studies and publication in foreign policy and popular journals like *Foreign Affairs* and the *Atlantic* and in opinion pieces in major newspapers in the United States and Europe.

It will help with international organizations like Amnesty International and Human Rights Watch, which have a strong interest in advancing human rights worldwide. So far these organizations have not focused their attention on the issue of Han-centrism and how it affects immigrants and the behavior of Chinese corporations abroad, especially in Africa.[54] These organizations do address some categories of Chinese human rights abuses, including highlighting the widespread use of capital punishment for crimes such as arson, embezzlement, and robbery. "Given the lack of an independent judiciary in China, the dominant role of the police, and the systematic overreliance on confessions—often extracted through torture—and the fact that thousands of cases are processed every year, there is a very real risk of miscarriages of justice," according to William Nee, the lead author of a 2017 Amnesty International study on capital punishment. China admits that until 2015 it used organs from executed prisoners for transplants, but now claims it relies on voluntary organ donation.[55]

Moreover, it allows the United States to advance a positive image in the international arena, to serve as an alternative and sharply contrasting image with China both now and in the future when the United States may be weaker than China. The connection to the global media is critical. Unfortunately, the constellation of power in global media will change with China's rise, especially since the Chinese are creating their own media and news services. *Financial Times, Times, the Guardian, the New York Times,* BBC, *Washington Post, Le Monde, Frankfurter Allgemeine Zeitung,* Fox and Sky News, CNN, and the other major networks will not always be dominant as the influence of nonwestern media grows, and so their ability to shape global opinion will be weakened. In contrast, China's media and the ability of China to advance its message will probably increase.

As Chinese power grows, the traditional alliance structures like NATO will come under greater strain, and even long-standing European allies may be tempted to jump on the bandwagon with China.[56] This will be so for three reasons. First, Beijing holds material power advantages, such as European debt, which gives them some influence over policy. It is important not to overstate this influence. Europe is far from captive, but some Chinese influence is undeniable. An important insight for

U.S. policy makers is that material power heavily informs fundamental interests of states, such as with whom it will ally. Of course, it is not solely determinative. People and states want to share interests and have a role in making decisions and to be treated as equals in the sense of having a role in institutional mechanisms and discussions. In general, the United States does this well; the Chinese do not.

Second, there is an ideological component. The attractiveness of the Beijing Consensus and socialism remains salient for a significant segment of the European population. For these Far Left Europeans, Beijing shows that socialism can work, and the train of reasoning for European socialists would be along these lines: "The revolutions of 1989 were an aberration due to the fact that the Soviets provided a false model of socialism. Socialism is redeemed through China's example, successful modernization, rise to dominance, and ultimate victory over capitalism." Of course, China has abandoned socialism in all but name. Yet for those on the European Left, the triumph of a nominally socialist China will be evidence of superiority of socialism and the failure of globalized capitalism.

Third, the legacy of anti-Americanism still exists in Europe. However, the culture of antiracism is very strong throughout European societies. Touting the salience of racism and the importance of combating racism will make it more difficult for European governments to distance them-selves from the United States in favor of an alliance with an ideologically incompatible China.

The "China is a hypernationalist state" message of the United States will help win allies in global culture, which is heavily influenced by ideals rooted in western political thought, including strong cultural and intellectual currents of antiracism. Recognizing that the West and its major institutions, the EU and NATO, are united by common political principles and a culture of antiracism yields an intellectual inheritance and ideological foundation for a unified front against China. In addition, popular cultural figures from film, music, television, and sports will be far better able to call attention to China's racism for younger audiences worldwide than will official or semiofficial Washington.

In sum, this is the "taking lemons and making lemonade" model. If it is the case that the United States is in decline or will be in the near future, it must use every effort to assist itself. It is to the advantage of the United States to have the world consider the costs of Chinese dominance in order to grasp what will be lost. This is an exercise that most of the world has not done, and so there is no appreciation of what will be lost or how hypocritical, domineering, and imperialistic China will be.

Han-Centrism Is a Cohesive Force for the Chinese

As with most matters in international politics, Han-centrism benefits the Chinese in four ways. First, the Han Chinese possess a strong in-group identity with a polarized and tightly defined out-group. They know who belongs and who does not. This allows the Chinese government to expect sacrifice as well as support and an acknowledgment of legitimacy from a considerable majority of the Chinese people.

Second, based on this identity, the government has the ability to focus with great willpower on the demands of the state. All governments make patriotic appeals, but the Chinese government is able to do so effectively because any entreaty is based on patriotism as well as nationalism.[57] Both Chinese patriotism and nationalism may be made fiercely with explicitly ethnocentric and xenophobic messages, emphasis on the Century of Humiliation, and appeals to ancestors and the civilizational identity of the Chinese. When we reflect on the tools the Chinese government uses to extract support and resources from the population, only one conclusion is possible: they are formidable.

Third, they have strong societal unity and purpose, which supports Chinese power. Dominant Chinese culture does not ponder its fundamental faults. When African American Sinologist M. Dujon Johnson considered his experiences in China and the Chinese inability to confront racism, he observed that Chinese culture "shies away from self and cultural criticism," and so he is not optimistic that a frank consideration of ethnocentrism and racism should ever be expected of China.[58]

While that can be a great strength for China, it also gives the United States an advantage. The lack of sufficient desire by the Chinese to address on the profound faults of their society means that there is no motivation to solve these faults. Accordingly, a powerful message may be that China will not change because it has no desire to do so. The country is a civilization, and that yields them great strength.

Of course, there also cannot be fundamental change in the near future. China is not an open society, transparent and porous for new ideas that would challenge its core beliefs. For those states and people whom the Chinese see as inferior, dissatisfaction with core beliefs is certain to increase as Chinese power expands. Thus the United States may tap into that "market of dissatisfaction" by calling attention to China's lack of flexibility, contempt for, and dismissal of the rest of the world.

Fourth, Han-centrism serves China's teleological worldview. History, in the Hegelian sense, is moving in China's direction, and the future belongs to it. China's political beliefs, civilizational culture, and economic power have triumphed over the West. This is Francis Fukuyama's "end of history" argument, except with China rather than the United States in the van of history. In essence, international politics is returning to "normal" with China at its center. This perception serves Chinese pride and provides them with a confidence reminiscent of that found in the West after the 1989 revolutions that swept Eastern Europe and the death of the Soviet Union. That is a powerful elixir for a people and one that is likely to fill the Chinese with even greater hubris that will offend and generate resentment throughout the world.

To advance its interests, the United States may make appeals to those actors in international politics who also do not want China to be at the center of the world, because their interests directly conflict with China's, like India, Japan, Vietnam, and even Russia; because they resent being excluded from consideration, treated unequally, or with disrespect; or because they reject China's selfish values and arrogant worldview.

Although it may be cold comfort for the United States, power in international politics is constantly being redistributed. China is rising today, but it may plateau or fall of its own devices, and this may occur in short order, perhaps more quickly and dramatically than could be expected or over a longer period of time.[59] Additionally, its power may be equalized or surpassed by the rise of other states like India. Indeed, perhaps an India allied with the United States and other partners will be able to prevent China from supplanting the United States. So China's rise is profound and one pregnant with many risks for the United States, but it also contains the certainty of decline. China may never get a chance to rule the world due to its own problems, the actions of its opponents, or both. Even if it does, its day, too, will end.

6   The Coming Struggle

What will happen when China really wakes up?
—Rudyard Kipling, *From Sea to Sea*

In 1889, while dining with British businessmen who were aiding in the economic and technological development of the Qing dynasty, Rudyard Kipling wondered aloud if it was wise to assist a country as potentially powerful as China. He deplored the men who were doing their best to "force upon the great Empire all the stimulants of the West—railways, tramlines, and so forth. What will happen when China really wakes up?"[1] The world now knows the answer to Kipling's question, which is complicated, as it inevitably is with the rise of great powers.

There are many positive elements associated with China's development. Indeed, on its own, each is awesome. Collectively, they are without parallel in the history of the world. The wealth created by China's growth has been a fillip to the global economy as well as its own. In a period measured only in decades, hundreds of millions of Chinese citizens have benefited. China's tremendous skill at executing major construction projects and building infrastructure has assisted states from Myanmar to the United Kingdom.

Of course, there is also the downside. The global community should be concerned about many elements that are likely to cause increasing friction. This study explored one of those. We considered the causes of

Han-centrism, its consequences for international politics, and how the United States might use this situation to its advantage. We commenced our argument in chapter 2, identifying Han-centrism as a form of hyper-nationalism and discussing its roots in the trauma and humiliation of the past two hundred years. By analyzing the political writings of Han nationalists during the late Qing dynasty and the 1911 Xinhai Revolution, such as Sun Yat-sen, Zhang Binglin, Zou Rong, and Liang Qichao, we saw how they constructed and articulated the cultural and ethnic symbols of Han identity and so gained a deeper understanding of how Han-centrism serves as an enduring dimension of Chinese nationalism. Finally, we considered the concept of race and found that Chinese religious-cultural and historical views of race reinforce Han-centrism. The Chinese see themselves as superior to the rest of the world.

Chapter 3 placed Han-centrism in a historical and contemporary context. We began by recognizing that Chinese nationalism exhibits many facets and can be fragmented, and so it is similar to nationalist beliefs held by many peoples and states throughout history. This chapter addressed the ways in which this identity was reproduced during the Mao period to support the CCP's national interests. We argued that Chinese nationalism has evolved from greater emphasis on the ideological foundation of Maoism to an ethnic one, based on Han identity.

What we see today is the CCP seeking to maintain legitimacy by making appeals to ethnic (Han) nationalist interests *and* promoting patriotism and national identity by emphasizing China's long history and the country's disempowerment during the Century of Humiliation. We argued that a by-product of the state-led nationalist education campaigns is not only a widespread cultural chauvinism that overwhelmingly pervades Chinese society, but also a growing number of "angry youth" who are helping fuel the growth of hypernationalism.

At the forefront of this movement are Han nationalists voicing their right to participate in Chinese politics. These aggressive nationalist counterclaims are, in part, attempting to shape the CCP's rewriting of historical memory, as well as influence the position China takes in regional and global politics. Han-centrism is promoted at the top by the political elite and at the bottom by nationalist elements found in the angry youth, settlers, bloggers, and the Chinese diaspora.

With this outgrowth of ethnic Han nationalism from above and below, we are witnessing the rise of Han-centric beliefs obsessed with the roots of Chinese weakness. The beliefs identify pernicious foreign influences as the cause of China's downfall in the past and the obstacle to regaining its historical position of power in international relations. The "foreigners" in this modern narrative are not just westerners but also internal foreigners, such as the various ethnic minorities within the country. Accordingly, we also evaluated the impact of manifestations of Han nationalism, including upon Africans in China, critics of the government and its Han-centric policies, and the Uighur minority and briefly addressed the deleterious consequences for these groups. Religion is not immune from Han-centrism's impact, and so this chapter also analyzed the long and complicated relationship between Christianity and the government of China.

Chapter 4 examined the impact of Han-centrism on Chinese foreign policy in particular and international politics in general. We found that it too frequently allows racist thought to be expressed in public. Elites are embracing this growth of popular nationalism and as a consequence are abandoning the "peaceful rise" discourse in favor of a more muscular approach inspired and justified by Han-centrism.

This makes it more likely that China will act aggressively, in accordance with hypernationalist visions of China's role in global politics, to avenge historical slights and insults and to advance its territorial demands. Han-centrism contributes to a strong, implicit, racial view of international relations that is alien and anathema to western policy makers and analysts. We argued that Han-centrism and Chinese strategic beliefs can affect Chinese crisis behavior in deleterious ways, including making it harder for the Chinese leadership to de-escalate in a crisis not only for hypernationalist reasons but also due to their concept of *shi*, or the strategic advantage that the Chinese expect themselves to possess. We also acknowledged that Han-centrism is beneficial for the Chinese leadership because it unites its citizens and so contributes to regime stability. The racial identity and collective memory associated with Han-centrism is a cohesive force that the Chinese political elite can exploit. China is not wracked with self-doubt or guilt about its past; rather, its history is lauded and self-affirming as the best of all civilizations.[2]

Finally, we presented two implications for international relations. First, China will make appeals to the Global South based on elements of racial solidarity and economics. Although these requests are made less frequently than they were during the Cold War, when they were a common trope in Maoist propaganda, they have not disappeared entirely. Second, despite these appeals, these entreaties are not completely effective and are even resisted due to the practical and unfavorable experiences that many states and businesses, particularly in Africa, but also Latin America and Southeast Asia, have had with the practices of the Chinese government and businesses.

In essence, Han-centrism hinders Chinese relations with the Global South. This makes it difficult to advance a sustainable positive message. Han-centric beliefs surface regularly in the Global South, and these beliefs, coupled with clannish and ruthless Chinese business practices, often generate enormous resentment in these states.

Chapter 5 considered China's soft power as a means to advancing its interests—its ability to provide aid, infrastructure with "few strings attached," and foreign investment with little political interference within the country or objections due to regime type. The international stage is set for the struggle between Beijing's model for development, capitalism wedded to authoritarianism, versus Washington's model of capitalism wedded to political freedom.

The chapter also presented the five major implications for U.S. decision makers and irregularities that may result from Han-centrism. Anchored in this discussion, we develop strategic asymmetries in the form of messages or themes based on these implications that the United States and its allies might advance to counter aspects of China's expanding position in international politics.

Asymmetrical Themes to Counter China's Growing Influence

While this study focused on China, in so doing, it obliquely provided a reflection on U.S. foreign relations. No doubt this is a difficult time for the United States. Its primacy in international politics is being challenged like never before by mounting fiscal difficulties, its numerous strategic challenges and military commitments, and China as a rising peer competitor. This combination makes it essential that the United States use every means available to maintain its strength. Calling attention to Han-centrism is one such strategy but nonetheless a powerful tool that provides the United States with leverage that will aid Washington in its effort to maintain its primacy and protect the liberal international order. These implications are summarized in table 2.

TABLE 2. Summary of asymmetries and themes that should be advanced

ASYMMETRIES/STRATEGIES	THEMES
1. Chinese hypernationalism provides evidence of how it will engage other international actors (i.e., China is the center of the universe; other societies are inferior).	A. The global community should conduct a reality check. B. China is unwilling to confront biases that stem from Han-centrism. C. The Han-centric worldview is flawed. D. China is a hypernationalistic superpower. The freedoms and tolerance characteristic of western societies are absent.

2. Undermine China in the Global South.	A. China has no culture of antiracism. B. Chinese business practices are destructive. C. China's "Third World Solidarity" diplomacy is hypocritical. D. The United States will uphold principles of racial equality and civil rights.
3. Promote a positive image of the United States to contrast with Chinese diplomacy and beliefs.	A. The United States has a history of welcoming immigrants who can prosper by contributing to the growth of American society. B. The United States is a free and open society. C. U.S. society does not tolerate racism in professional life and seeks to minimize it, while maximizing equality (i.e., affirmative action).
4. Foster political and ideological alliances with states that oppose China's Han-centric worldview, especially in Europe and the Global South.	A. Sympathetic popular culture figures should be brought in to assist in drawing attention to Chinese beliefs and destructive policies in the developing world. B. The EU and NATO are united in a culture of antiracism, common political norms, principles, and values. This serves as a normative foundation for an alliance against China. C. The reality of imperialistic Chinese dominance is highlighted in international politics.
5. Han-centrism leads to strong in-group identity, successful patriotic appeals, societal unity, and purpose without culture of criticism of its fundamental faults.	A. China has no desire to adjust/ change its nationalistic worldview. B. China is a closed society in contrast to the United States. C. China will not go through a civil rights movement or develop a strong culture of antiracism in the near future. D. China's Han-centric values and worldview threaten the national interests of allies and smaller powers.

The Han-Centric Worldview

Han-centrism provides empirical evidence of how the Chinese will treat other international actors if China becomes dominant. One of the key insights into future behavior is China's behavior in the past when it was the hegemon of Asia, the known world as far as China was concerned. China sees itself as the center of the universe. All others are inferior, although there are varying degrees of inferiority. That is not an attractive model for winning friends and maintaining alliance structures.

The United States and its allies might advance the following themes to weaken China's global position. The Chinese have a huge burden imposed on them by their Han-centrism, and it will surface inevitably in their dealings with the rest of the world. As they become more powerful, they will be less restrained about evincing these behaviors and alienating their critics. The first of these themes should be to advance a "reality check" to the global community. "How do Chinese words match Chinese deeds when it comes to treating people fairly and equally?"

The second theme is to introduce fault. "Why has the Chinese government done so little to hinder the xenophobia, chauvinism, and racism of Han nationalism?" Or more succinctly, "Why is China an exclusionary state—a closed society, with severe limits on immigration and human rights?" Attention needs to be called to its eugenics policies as well. "Why do the Chinese support eugenics decades after it was discredited in the West?" Too often racist beliefs and eugenics inform Chinese perceptions of the world. Most often, the Chinese do not even recognize that eugenics and racism are problems, believing that racism is a western phenomenon and that westerners are obsessed with it.

A third theme is to suggest that there is something profoundly wrong: "Why are the Chinese unable to change their worldviews?" Or there is something fundamentally wrong with Chinese society or with their political elite: "Racism has been confronted worldwide. Why is it so often ignored and tolerated in Chinese society?"

These themes allow the United States and other states to challenge China's projected image of an oppressed victim of racism with empirical reality. China is a hypernationalistic superpower. It is quite unlike the free and tolerant societies found in the West.

China's Treatment of the Global South

Han-centrism allows the United States to undermine China in less developed nations. The United States needs to counter the expansion of Chinese influence by tying in to the messages stated above, but adding the important point that there is no culture of opposition to hypernationalism or antiracism in China, and so there is little hope for change. Messages may be advanced along the following line: "The West confronted hypernationalism and racism in its societies and developed a strong culture to combat both, yet China has not, nor is it likely to do so."

The United States should argue that Chinese business practices are ruthless and destructive. There often is considerable resentment toward Chinese practices that undercut and destroy African businesses and marginalize local communities. The combination of the two messages, "China's unwillingness to confront racism has resulted in aggressive businesses practices that are destructive for the locals," would be most effective in making appeals to the Global South.

Third, it is an obvious point, but it must be made: the Chinese are hypocrites when it comes to racial equality. For all of their rhetoric on Africa and their "African brothers," the cold facts outweigh paeans to "Third World solidarity."

Fourth, the message of the United States should be "We are better for Africa than the Chinese. We will assist you with economic aid to offset what you receive from China. Culturally, socially, and politically, we are better, we are equal, and we recognize racial equality and civil rights."

Advancement of a Positive U.S. Image

When compared with China, it is easy to convey the message to the rest of the world that the United States is open and inclusive, whereas China is not. This fact provides a significant advantage for the United States.

The messages should be, first, the United States seeks the best from around the world and will permit them to come to the country so that they may prosper and, in turn, aid the economic growth and innovation of American society. Second, the United States opens its society, educational system, universities, military, and economy to immigrants, as countless examples demonstrate. Third, it has in place affirmative action policies as a matter of state policy that benefit immigrants from racial minorities and/or those who are women. In sum, the United States is one of the most transparent societies in the world for immigrants.

Strengthening U.S. Alliances

Calling attention to Han-centrism allows the United States to strengthen political and ideological alliances, especially in the Global South. Equally important are the ideological alliances that the United States may augment. Intellectual circles in Europe, Canada, and the United States value multiracial and multicultural societies. Recognizing that the West and its major institutions, the EU and NATO, are united by common political principles and a shared culture of antiracism establishes a shared intellectual inheritance and ideological foundation for a unified front against China. This will become increasingly important as the Atlantic alliance comes under increasing strain due to the growth of Chinese power. Thus touting the salience of Han-centrism and the importance of combating racism will make it more difficult for European governments to distance themselves from the United States in favor of an alliance with an ideologically incompatible China.

Journalists and media opinion makers frequently share a multiracial and multicultural vision of their societies as well. Yet they have not treated the problem of Han-centrism and its inherent racism with the attention it deserves. The "Bad ideas dominate in China" message of the United States will help win allies in global, popular culture, which is heavily influenced by ideals rooted in western political thought, including strong currents of civil rights. Popular cultural figures from film, music, television, and sports will be far better able to call attention to China's racism for younger audiences worldwide than will official or semiofficial Washington.

It is to the advantage of the United States to have the world consider the costs of Chinese dominance in order to grasp what will be lost. This is an exercise that most of the world has not begun, and so there is no appreciation of how hypocritical, domineering, and imperialistic China will be.

Advantages Based on Han-Centrism

Finally, the United States and its allies must recognize that Han-centrism is a cohesive force for the Chinese. It benefits them in four ways. First, the Han Chinese possess a strong in-group identity with a polarized and tightly defined out-group. This allows their government to expect sacrifice as well as support from the majority of citizens.

Second, based in this identity, the government has the ability to focus on the demands of the state. All governments make patriotic appeals, but the Chinese government is able to do so effectively because any entreaty is based on nationalism. When we reflect on the tools the Chinese government has to extract support and resources from the population, only one conclusion is possible: they are formidable.

Third, they have strong societal unity and purpose, which supports Chinese power. Under the CCP, the Chinese do not have a culture that is self-critical or one that ponders its fundamental faults. China's hypernationalism serves its teleological worldview. History, in the Hegelian sense, is moving in China's direction, the future belongs to it, and China's political beliefs, civilizational culture, and economic power will triumph over the West.

While Han-centrism can be a great strength for China, it also gives the United States an advantage. The lack of any desire by the Chinese to reflect on the profound faults of their society means that there is no motivation to mend these flaws. Accordingly, a powerful message may be that China will not change because it has no desire to do so.

At the same time, there cannot be fundamental change. China is not an open society, transparent and porous for new ideas that would challenge its core beliefs. For those states and peoples whom the Chinese see as inferior, dissatisfaction with core Chinese beliefs is certain to increase as Chinese power expands. Thus the United States may tap into that "market of dissatisfaction" by calling attention to China's lack of flexibility as well as its contempt for and dismissal of the rest of the world.

Western attitudes on race have changed over the last two generations through the creation of civil rights movements and strong cultures of antiracism. These positive developments bode well for western societies, but given the possibility of western decline in the face of increased Chinese power, there is also cause for concern. The world may witness the rise of a superpower where bigoted views are accepted as a legitimate part of public discourse. This is significant because the fundamental question for the future of peace and stability in international politics is how China sees the rest of the world and whether the norms that the West has created, particularly against racism and exploitation, could be maintained under Chinese hegemony. Knowing what the Chinese think of race, the answer is not positive for maintaining a global culture of antiracism.

Directly put, the issue is whether China can ever establish a culture of antiracism. It is unlikely that the Chinese would ever transform their society through a civil rights movement like the United States. First, they have no freedom of the press, freedom to petition their government, or freedom to assemble, all of which are necessary to support a civil rights movement. Second, there is no political drive or consciousness for equality. Equality is associated with Maoism and rejected in today's China, where inequality is widespread. In addition, there really is no notion of civil rights in Chinese jurisprudence.

These elements unite to force the conclusion that there is little likelihood that the Chinese attitudes toward race will change. There is little to no force from below, no popular movement demanding minority rights, to compel them to do so. Equally, there is no motivation to force such an adjustment from above.

By contrast, the western political systems are open to profound adaptation and correction and have demonstrated the ability to make significant reforms in civil and human rights over time. There is ample proof of the West's more adaptive and inclusive political system. For example, the United States removed the principal obstacles to equality for African Americans and other racial minorities with *Brown v. Board of Education* in 1954 and the Civil Rights and Voting Rights Acts of 1964 and 1965. In addition, the Immigration Act of 1965 opened the possibility of immigration to the United States for people previously excluded because of race. The U.S. government has labored mightily to improve the condition of all minorities within its borders through official policies backed by cultural and other forces, such as the media, the educational system, and the influence of Hollywood and popular culture.

Lastly, the United States may make appeals to those actors in international politics who do not desire China to be at the center of the world either, first, because their interests directly conflict with China's, like India, Japan, Russia, and Vietnam; second, because they resent being excluded from consideration, treated unequally or with disrespect; or third, because they reject China's Han-centric values. These insights provide a significant opening for the United States to advance its interests at China's expense.

A New Global Struggle

Our conclusion is that endemic Han-centrism offers the United States a reason to work with major countries and foreign leaders. The United States is on the right side in the struggle against hypernationalistic beliefs, and China is not. The U.S government, allies, and academics should call attention to this to aid Washington's position in international politics.

The United States must be confident and strong enough to advance these messages against China. The West does have significant influence in China and should use its power to advance its interests. It is to be expected that the Chinese government will always protest, and do so rather vociferously, any statement of fact concerning Han-centrism, its hypernationalistic and racist components, or criticism as interference in China's internal affairs.

It deserves to be stated plainly that the fate of the country depends to a large extent on decisions made in the West. The eminent economist Guy Sorman stresses this vulnerability when he argues: "Should foreign investment and imports begin to peter out, the Chinese economy would come to a grinding halt."[3] This is because "sixty percent of Chinese exports are carried out by foreign companies, and the Communist Party's survival depends on its ability to maintain a favored relationship with Western decision makers," and "it is precisely for this reason that the Propaganda Department assiduously woos Western public opinion and tries to buy it off."[4]

As Chinese dissident Wei Jingsheng [魏京生] argues, the fear of losing the vast Chinese market turns business and governmental leaders into cowards. However, this myopia will not last long: "Sooner or later, the Americans will realize that the Communist Party has been lying to them about everything be it intellectual property, human rights, Taiwan, or its support to North Korea."[5] The critical question implied by Sorman should be stated in clear terms: "Is a conflict between the United States and China inevitable?" For Wei, "A showdown is inevitable with the Communist Party but not with the Chinese people." He reminds us that so far, twenty-six dynasties have ruled over China. "Now the time for democracy has come."[6]

One need not share Wei's optimistic view of the prospects of democracy in China to be greatly concerned about the possibility of conflict between China and the United States. In a period of increasing security competition with China, the United States needs to take stock of all of its advantages and resources. To advance its interests, the United States may make appeals to those actors in international politics, and India is foremost, that do not desire China to be at the center of the world either. A large part of this confrontation will be in the realm of ideas, diplomacy, popular culture, and public opinion of U.S. allies, the Global South, and in China itself.

Fundamentally, the great advantage is that the United States is a better society than China and a better manager of the interests of allies and the global community. The United States has done far more for the world through its creation of the global economic order, its many humanitarian actions, and the stability that results from its military alliances and power. It is an open, transparent society that welcomes foreigners and permits them to enjoy full civil rights and the prodigious benefits of living in a democracy.

Unfortunately, facts will not speak for themselves. As this study has demonstrated, there is a great reluctance by many actors to point out the profound consequences of Han-centrism. If this is going to be accomplished, it must be done through a concerted effort. This study is the first contribution to that goal. At the same time, the United States needs to proclaim its considerable strengths to other nations. It needs to tap into the resentment that China generates inexorably through its rapid growth and the inevitable strategic hubris and mistakes that accompany such a spectacular rise.

Additional research should be conducted, first, to explore how the messages may be tailored, expanded, or modified to reach all global audiences; second, to illuminate other societal weaknesses China possesses that may serve as asymmetries for the United States in its global competition with China; and third, to understand what other strengths the United States possesses, whether these are societal or other new tools that may be used in the confrontation.

Finally, it must be stated directed: China is a hypernationalistic state and very proud of this fact. This must be recognized to compel all international actors—states, nongovernment organizations, human rights groups, academics, media, celebrities, and individuals—to think through the consequences of the rise of China for what they believe and value and how China's ascent will affect their beliefs and values. The commercial lure of China is strong, and the Sino-American competition has many components. But one neglected aspect needs to be highlighted. The Sino-American confrontation has a moral component, too. It needs to be thought of as a clash between right and wrong, an open society and a closed one. Just as in the Cold War, the United States is on the right side.

NOTES

1. THE PROBLEM OF HAN-CENTRISM

1. Scholars have developed theories and approaches to this question. Power transition theory yields insights into past hegemonic struggles; neorealism, neoliberalism, and constructivism also provide understanding, as do theories of foreign policy analysis and bureaucratic behavior. Sinologists provide additional approaches that yield significant judgments and discernments into Chinese motivations and likely future actions. For example, see He, *China's Crisis Behavior*; Pillsbury, *Hundred-Year Marathon*; and Shambaugh, *China Goes Global*.

2. Broomfield, "Perceptions of Danger"; Halper, *Beijing Consensus*; Jacques, *When China Rules the World*; Ross, "Assessing the China Threat"; and Roy, "The 'China Threat' Issue."

3. For example, see Christiansen, "A Liberal Institutionalist Perspective"; Glaser, "Will China's Rise Lead to War?"; Ikenberry, "The Rise of China and the Future of the West"; Johnston, "Is China a Status Quo Power?" 5–56.

4. Weiss, *Powerful Patriots*; Fewsmith and Rosen, "Domestic Context of Chinese Foreign Policy"; Gries, "Chinese Nationalism"; Hughes, "Nationalism and Multilateralism"; and Reilly, "A Wave to Worry About?"

5. Agnew, "Looking Back to Look Forward"; Rozman, "Chinese National Identity"; Townsend, "Chinese Nationalism"; and S. Zhao, "Chinese Nationalism."

6. Yang and Zheng, "*Fen Qings* (Angry Youth)."

7. Blanchard and Slodkowski, "China Marks 'National Humiliation Day' with Anti-Japanese Protests."

8. Weiss, "Authoritarian Signaling, Mass Audiences"; Gries, Steiger, and Wang, "Popular Nationalism and China's Japan Policy"; and Reilly, "A Wave to Worry About?"

9. Carrico and Gries, "Nations and Nationalism Roundtable Discussion," 431.

10. Van Evera, "Hypotheses on Nationalism and War."

11. Baranovitch, "Others No More"; Berry, "'Race' (民族)"; Gladney, *Dislocating China*; and Hood, "Distancing Disease in the Un-Black Han Chinese Politic."
12. Chow, "Imagining Boundaries of Blood"; Lin, "Policies and Practices of Bilingual Education for the Minorities in China."
13. While China's rise will continue, its economic growth is slowing. Natural depredations like growing resource scarcities, environmental destruction, and widespread pollution, as well as broad economic and social problems such as ubiquitous corruption, which undermines aspects of the economy like the banking system, a collapse of trust in personal and commercial relationships, gross disparities in income and regional development, and economic bubbles in property, concrete, and steel conspire to reduce economic growth. Moreover, China's demography is also problematic. China faces a "triple whammy": the number of children under fourteen will fall by 53 million by 2050, the workforce will contract by 100 million, and those over sixty will rise by 234 million, from 12 percent to 31 percent of the population. The gender imbalance, male births exceed female births by 106:100 worldwide, but in China the ratio is 124:100. The social impact of this imbalance is significant as marriage competition intensifies, with increasing alienation of unmarried males. As a consequence of its demographics alone, China's growth rates are decelerating, even if they remain impressive by the standards of the rest of the world. However, it is also the case that the reduced cost of automation yields a reduction in unskilled labor unemployment, so the reduced population and reduced labor demand may be partially offset.
14. G. Smith, "Chinese Reactions to Anti-Asian Riots in the Pacific."
15. Kaltman, *Under the Heel of the Dragon*, 128.
16. Rennie, "The Lion and the Dragon," 379, 391.
17. Z. Wang, "National Humiliation, History Education."
18. Kaufman, "Xi Jinping as Historian: Marxist, Chinese, Nationalist, Global"; Friedman, "Raising Sheep on Wolf Milk"; Shen and Breslin, *Online Chinese Nationalism and China's Bilateral Relations*.
19. Weiss, "Popular Protest, Nationalism."
20. For example, see Gries, Steiger, and Wang, "Popular Nationalism and China's Japan Policy."
21. Whitmeyer, "Elites and Popular Nationalism."
22. For example, Agnew identifies four major Chinese conceptions of its place in the world: The "Pacific Rim," which centers on China's relationship with overseas Chinese and neighboring countries; the "Orientalist" vision which sees a Chinese exceptionalism anchored in a Sinocentric tributary system; the "nationalist *geopolitik*," which focuses on China's need to protect access to resources around

the world through sea power; and an "international relations with Chinese characteristics," which mines Chinese history to develop a Chinese theory of international politics based on a benevolent nature of Chinese power and how international politics might be reorganized along Chinese rather than Westphalian principles. See Agnew, "Looking Back to Look Forward." An important and related argument, strongly emphasizing China's geopolitical turn, is Hughes, "Reclassifying Chinese Nationalism."

23. Of course, conflict between China and the United States is not destiny. There are measures both states may take to reduce the risk of conflict. However, we expect based on our argument and other avenues to conflict that increased security competition is probable.

24. For a review of these causes, see Thayer, "Humans, Not Angels."

25. See Blainey, *Causes of Wars*; Hutchinson, *Nationalism and War*; and Van Evera, *Causes of War*.

26. S. Zhao, "China's Pragmatic Nationalism."

27. After having examined the literature on Chinese nationalism and Han-centrism extensively, among the best analyses are Joniak-Lüthi, *The Han*; Weatherly, *Making China Strong*; and Wu, *Chinese Cyber Nationalism*.

28. Dikötter's work has addressed the issue of nationalism and racism in China most directly in his *Discourse of Race in Modern China* and *Construction of Racial Identities in China and Japan*. More distantly and obliquely touching on the topic is Michael Keevak, *Becoming Yellow* and Jacques, *When China Rules the World*. One African American Sinologist has offered his reflections on blatant Chinese racism toward African Americans in particular is M. Johnson, *Race and Racism in the Chinas*.

29. Kowner and Demel, "Modern East Asia and the Rise of Racial Thought."

30. Tang and Darr, "Chinese Nationalism and Its Political and Social Origins," 814.

31. S. Zhao, "Foreign Policy Implications of Chinese Nationalism Revisited."

32. Baranovitch, "Others No More."

33. Chu, "The Power of Knowledge."

34. Patent, "China," 174.

35. Tuttle, "China's Problem with Race," 39.

36. Tang and Darr, "Chinese Nationalism and Its Political and Social Origins," 820. See also Shirk, *China: Fragile Superpower*.

37. Gonzalez-Vicente, "The Empire Strikes Back?" 1–3.

38. French, *China's Second Continent*.

39. Carlson, "A Flawed Perspective."

40. Johnston, "Is Chinese Nationalism Rising?"

41. Z. Wang, "National Humiliation, History Education." Also see Daniel Sneider, "Textbooks and Patriotic Education."

42. Zhongguo geming bowuguan [Revolutionary History Museum of China], *Zhongguo: Cong quru zouxiang huihuang.*

43. Han, *Micro-Blogging Memories*, 122.

44. Callahan, "National Insecurities," 200.

45. Dikötter, *Discourse of Race in Modern China*, 71.

46. Zeng, *Chinese Communist Party's Capacity to Rule*; Weiss, *Powerful Patriots.*

47. Gries, Steiger, and Wang, "Popular Nationalism and China's Japan Policy."

48. Jia, "Disrespect and Distrust."

49. Costa, "Focusing on Chinese Nationalism."

50. Woods and Dickson, "Victims and Patriots," 180.

51. Zarrow, "Historical Trauma"; Laitinen, *Chinese Nationalism in the Late Qing Dynasty*; and Leibold, "Xinhai Remembered."

2. THE ORIGINS OF HAN-CENTRISM

1. A. Smith, *Ethno-Symbolism and Nationalism*; Anderson, *Imagined Communities.*

2. Hall, "The Question of Cultural Identity," 299.

3. Wade, "Racial Identity and Nationalism"; Parker et al., *Nationalisms and Sexualities*, 5.

4. Carlson, "A Flawed Perspective."

5. Leibold, "Competing Narratives of Racial Unity in Republican China," 184.

6. Van Evera, "Hypotheses on Nationalism and War."

7. Van Evera, "Primed for Peace."

8. Kaufman, "An 'International' Theory of Inter-Ethnic War"; Peterson, *Understanding Ethnic Violence.*

9. Bertrand, *Nationalism and Ethnic Conflict in Indonesia*, 11.

10. Kaufman, "Escaping the Symbolic Politics Trap," 202.

11. Gagnon, "Ethnic Nationalism and International Conflict"; Hagan, "Domestic Political Systems and War Proneness."

12. Spencer, "Collective Violence and Everyday Practice in Sri Lanka."

13. Sahdra and Ross, "Group Identification and Historical Memory," 385.

14. For example, see Ashplant, Dawson, and Roper, *Politics of War Memory and Commemoration*; Saito, *History Problem.*

15. Smith, *National Identity.*

16. Cairns and Roe, "Introduction: Why Memories in Conflict?."

17. Horowitz, *Ethnic Groups in Conflict*, 59.

18. Brubaker, "Ethnicity, Race, and Nationalism."

19. Eller, *From Culture to Ethnicity to Conflict*, 29, 47.

20. Ahmed, "'Ethnic Cleansing.'"
21. Blagojevic, "Causes of Ethnic Conflict."
22. Wade, "Racial Identity and Nationalism," 848.
23. Halbwachs, *On Collective Memory*, 25.
24. Z. Wang, *Never Forget National Humiliation*; Callahan, "National Insecurities"; Gries, *China's New Nationalism*.
25. Z. Wang, *Never Forget National Humiliation*.
26. Chow, "Narrating Nation, Race, and National Culture," 49.
27. Cited in Karl, *Staging the World*, 13.
28. Z. Wang, *Never Forget National Humiliation*, 68.
29. Harrison, *Making of the Republican Citizen*. Also see Mishar, *From the Ruins of Empire*.
30. Karl, *Staging the World*.
31. Teng and Fairbank, *China's Response to the West*.
32. Rhoads, *Manchus and Han*.
33. Zarrow, "Historical Trauma"; Laitinen, *Chinese Nationalism in the Late Qing Dynasty*; Leibold, "Xinhai Remembered."
34. Y. Wong, *Search for Modern Nationalism*, 62.
35. Edwards, "Narratives of Race and Nation in China."
36. Zou, *Revolutionary Army*, 65.
37. Zarrow, "Historical Trauma," 72, 77.
38. Zarrow: *After Empire*, 160; Pillemer, "Psychology of Memory" 145.
39. Cited in Zarrow, *After Empire*, 163.
40. Cited in Pillemer, "Psychology of Memory" 145.
41. On the concept of ethnic emotions, see Blagojevic, "Causes of Ethnic Conflict."
42. Pillemer, "Psychology of Memory," 146–47.
43. Brubaker, "Ethnicity, Race, and Nationalism," 25, 29.
44. Fiskesjö, "Rescuing the Empire."
45. Duara, *Rescuing History from the Nation*, 15
46. Dikötter, *Discourse of Race*, 74.
47. Dikötter, *Construction of Racial Identity*, 6.
48. Dikötter, *Discourse of Race*, 61.
49. Balibar and Wallerstein, *Race, Nation, and Class*, 54.
50. Duara, *Rescuing History from the Nation*.
51. G. Zhao, "Reinventing China," 3–30.
52. Elliott, *Manchu Way*.
53. Zarrow, *After Empire*, 157.
54. Leibold, "Xinhai Remembered."
55. Zou, *Revolutionary Army*, 58.

56. Cited in Teng and Fairbank, *China's Response to the West*, 267–68.
57. Chow, "Narrating Nation, Race, and National Culture." Also see Leibold, "Competing Narratives of Racial Unity."
58. Rhoads, *Manchus and Han*.
59. Rawski, "Presidential Address."
60. Cheek, *Intellectual in Modern Chinese History*.
61. Chung, "Better Science and Better Race?" 795.
62. Duara, *Rescuing History from the Nation*, 139, 140–41.
63. Dikötter, "Racial Identity in China: Context and Meaning."
64. H. Yang, "Encountering Darwin and Creating Darwinism in China."
65. Dikötter, *Discourse of Race in Modern China*, 68.
66. Rhoads, *Manchus and Han*, 2.
67. Dikötter, "Racial Identity in China."
68. Jacques, *When China Rules the World*; Jia, "Disrespect and Distrust."
69. Zou, *The Revolutionary Army*, 106.
70. Leibold, "Competing Narratives of Racial Unity," 186.
71. Harris, "Chinese Nationalism," 124.
72. Dikötter, *Discourse of Race in Modern China*, 69.
73. Cited in Pusey, *China and Charles Darwin*, 117.
74. Cited in Villard, "'Class,' 'Race,' and Language," 316.
75. H. Yang, "Encountering Darwin and Creating Darwinism in China."
76. Cited in B. Schwartz, *In Search of Wealth and Power*, 55.
77. S-C Shen, "Discourse on Guomin ('the Citizen') in Late Qing China," 8.
78. Teng and Fairbank, *China's Response to the West*, 228.
79. Cited in Schell and Delury, *Wealth and Power*, 131.
80. Sun, *The Three Principles of the People*, 4–5.
81. Teng and Fairbank, *China's Response to the West*, 227.
82. Dikötter, *Discourse of Race in Modern China*, 71.
83. Zarrow, *After Empire*, 173; Leibold, "Competing Narratives of Racial Unity."
84. Sautman, "Racial Nationalism and China's External Behavior."
85. Schell and Delury, *Wealth and Power*, 131.
86. Duara, *Rescuing History from the Nation*, 141, 35.
87. Rawski, "Presidential Address," 841. See also Duara, *Rescuing History from the Nation*, and Townsend, "Chinese Nationalism."
88. Sautman, "Racial Nationalism and China's External Behavior."

3. HAN-CENTRISM IN CHINESE HISTORY AND TODAY

1. Duara, *Rescuing History from the Nation*, 4.
2. Zheng, *Discovering Chinese Nationalism in China*, 113.

3. Feng, "Nationalism and Democratisation in Contemporary China"; Liu, *No Enemies, No Hatred.*

4. Y. Guo, "Patriotic Villains and Patriotic Heroes."

5. Lai, *Nativism and Modernity.*

6. Seckington, "Nationalism, Ideology, and China's 'Fourth Generation' Leadership." Also see Schram, *Political Thought of Mao Tse-tung.*

7. Fairbank, *Chinese World Order*; Fairbank, "Tributary Trade and China's Relations with the West"; Zhang, "The Rise of Chinese Exceptionalism in International Relations."

8. Barmé, "To Screw Foreigners Is Patriotic," 211.

9. Howland, "The Dialectics of Chauvinism," 177.

10. Zhang, "Chinese Exceptionalism in the Intellectual World of China's Foreign Policy."

11. Chen, *Mao's China and the Cold War*, 237.

12. Li, "Guanyu Minzu gongzuozhong de jige wenti" [On Some Questions Encountered in the Nationality Work, September 1961], 366–68.

13. On this point, Mao wrote: "In some places the relations between nationalities are far from normal. For Communists, this is an intolerable situation. We must go to the root and criticize the Han chauvinist ideas which exist to a serious degree among many Party members and cadres, namely, the reactionary ideas of the landlord class and the bourgeoisie, or the ideas characteristic of the Guomindang, which are manifested in the relations between nationalities." See Mao, "Pipan da Hanzu Zhuyi" [Inner-party directive drafted for the Central Committee of the CCP, March 16, 1953], 87.

14. Howland, "Dialectics of Chauvinism," 190.

15. Howland, "Dialectics of Chauvinism," 188.

16. Rossabi, *Governing China's Multiethnic Frontiers*, 8.

17. Howland, "Dialectics of Chauvinism," 172.

18. Rossabi, *Governing China's Multiethnic Frontiers*, 8.

19. Zheng, *Discovering Chinese Nationalism in China.*

20. Unger, *Chinese Nationalism*, xi; Link, "China's 'Core' Problem."

21. Guo, "Patriotic Villains and Patriotic Heroes," 164.

22. Bernstein and Munro, "Coming Conflict with America"; Lilley, "Nationalism Bites Back." For a helpful discussion of Confucianism, see Kuhn, *Age of Confucian Rule*, and Pines, *Everlasting Empire*. Insightful as well is Y-K Wang, *Harmony and War.*

23. Zhang, "The Rise of Chinese Exceptionalism in International Relations," 307.

24. Callahan, *China*; Duara, *Rescuing History from the Nation.*

25. Gilley, *Tiger on the Brink*; S. Zhao, "A State-Led Nationalism."

26. Weatherly, *Making China Strong*, 184.

27. Friedman, "Raising Sheep on Wolf Milk," 389–409; Z. Wang, *Never Forget National Humiliation,*

28. Gries, "Chinese Nationalism."

29. Z. Wang, "National Humiliation."

30. Z. Wang, "National Humiliation."

31. Friedman, "Raising Sheep on Wolf Milk."

32. "The CCP Central Committee's Notification about Issuing 'The Implementation Outline of Patriotic Education.'"

33. People's Republic of China, Ministry of Education, *Teaching Guideline for History Education* [历史教学大纲].

34. Buckley, "China Warns Officials against 'Dangerous' Western Values."

35. Economy, "China's Imperial President."

36. Levin, "China Tells Schools to Suppress Western Ideas, with One Big Exception."

37. "Yuan Guiren: University Teachers Must Maintain Political, Legal, and Moral Bottom Lines."

38. Harris, "Chinese Nationalism."

39. Duara, *Culture, Power, and the State*; Fitzgerald, "The Nationless State"; Tan and Chen, "China's Competing and Co-opting Nationalisms."

40. Bislev, "Nationalist Netizens in China," 118; Gries, "Chinese Nationalism."

41. S. Shen, "Nationalism or Nationalist Foreign Policy?"; Yang and Zheng, "*Fen Qings* (Angry Youth)."

42. Friedman, "Raising Sheep on Wolf Milk"; Xu, "Chinese Populist Nationalism."

43. S-D Liu, "China's Popular Nationalism on the Internet," 144–55; Tang and Darr, "Chinese Nationalism and Its Political and Social Origins."

44. Gries, "Chinese Nationalism"; Friedman, "Raising Sheep on Wolf Milk."

45. Weiss, *Powerful Patriots*; Reilly, "A Wave to Worry About?"

46. Yu, "Glorious Memories of Imperial China."

47. Duara, "De-constructing the Chinese Nation"; Townsend, "Chinese Nationalism."

48. Chase, "Nationalism and the Net"; Horesh et al., "Is My Rival's Rival a Friend?"; Yahuda, "China's New Assertiveness in the South China Sea."

49. Gries, "Koguryo Controversy."

50. Wong, "Xi Again Defends China's Claim to the South China Sea Islands."

51. Rauhala and Denyer, "Chinese State Media Melt Down over South China Sea Ruling."

52. J. Guo, "Different Images of Putin."

53. Bislev, "Nationalist Netizens in China."

54. Wong, "In New China, 'Hostile' West Is Still Derided."

55. Zhou Xiaoping, "Nine Knockout Blows in America's Cold War against China."
56. Leibold, "Han Cybernationalism and State Territorialization," 4–11, 14.
57. Pan, *Out of Mao's Shadow*, 323. See also Holbig and Gilley, "Reclaiming Legitimacy in China."
58. Rozman, "Chinese National Identity," 95.
59. Wertime and Hui, "Is This the New Face of China's Silent Majority?" and Wong, "In New China, 'Hostile' West is Still Derided."
60. Chew and Wang, "Online Cultural Conservatism and Han Ethnicism in China."
61. While a detailed discussion is beyond the scope of our study, we recognize that the term "Chinese Dream" has contrasting interpretations, the most important of which are Xi's and Liu Mingfu's. For an example consistent with their interpretation, see "Inherit the Past, Usher in the Future, Continue to Press Forward to the Goal of Chinese Nation's Great Rejuvenation."
62. Economy, "China's Imperial President."
63. "Xi Stresses Continuation of Native Culture."
64. For an excellent discussion of Sun Yat-sen's revolutionary role, see Sun, *Memoirs of a Chinese Revolutionary*; and Sun, *The Three Principles of Democracy*. Also see Chang and Gordon, *All under Heaven*; and Cohen, *Speaking to History*.
65. Leibold, "Xinhai Remembered."
66. Zhao, "Chinese Nationalism and Its International Orientations."
67. Chew and Wang, "Online Cultural Conservativism and Han Ethnicism in China," 3.
68. Zhao and Postiglione, "Representations of Ethnic Minorities in China's University Media."
69. Leibold, "More than a Category," 549.
70. Callahan, *China*.
71. Baranovitch, "Others No More," 85–122; Berry, "'Race' (民族)"; Gladney, *Dislocating China*; Hood, "Distancing Disease in the Un-Black Han Chinese Politic."
72. Lin, "Policies and Practices of Bilingual Education for the Minorities in China."
73. Hasmath, "The Interactions of Ethnic Minorities in Beijing," 9.
74. Agnew, "Looking Back to Look Forward," 305.
75. Martin Jacques provides an insightful overview of the discrimination against Uighurs and Tibetans in *When China Rules the World*, 244–56. Excellent accounts remain J. Dreyer, *China's Forty Millions*, and Heberer, *China and Its National Minorities*.
76. Blanchard, "China Lauds Minority Rights on Key Anniversary," Reuters, August 8, 2007, quoted in Marriott and Lacroix, *Fault Lines on the Face of China*, 95.

77. Chew and Wang, "Online Cultural Conservativism and Han Ethnicism in China," 4.
78. Friedrichs, "Sino-Muslim Relations." Also see Hyer, "China's Policy towards Uighur Nationalism" and "Sinocentricism and the National Question in China."
79. Han, "Boundaries, Discrimination, and Interethnic Conflict in Xinjiang," 254.
80. "Settlers in Xinjiang: Circling the Wagons." Also see, Bovingdon, *Autonomy in Xinjiang*, and Jacobs, "Xinjiang Seethes under Chinese Crackdown."
81. Quoted in "Wild West," 15.
82. "Wild West," 16–17.
83. These incidents are described in "Wild West," 15–17.
84. "Xinjiang: Fast and Loose."
85. "Wild West," 16–17.
86. Quoted in "Xinjiang: Fast and Loose."
87. Bodeen, "Beijing Report Says Chinese Muslims Are in Syria."
88. Bovingdon, *Autonomy in Xinjiang*, and Jacobs, "Xinjiang Seethes under Chinese Crackdown."
89. Irwin, "Why Is China Banning Baby Names and Beards in Xinjiang?"
90. Cheng, "From Campus Racism to Cyber Racism," 562.
91. Hevi, *An African Student in China*.
92. M. Johnson, *Race and Racism in the Chinas*, 27, 131.
93. Chow, "Narrating Nation, Race, and National Culture."
94. Wimmer, "Explaining Xenophobia and Racism."
95. Xu, "Chinese Populist Nationalism," 122.
96. Chew and Wang, "Online Cultural Conservativism and Han Ethnicism in China."
97. Frazier and Zhang, "Ethnic Identity and Racial Contestation in Cyberspace," 239.
98. For examples of Han-centrism on Baidu Tieba, see the following forums: "Rejuvenate Han and Develop China, Strive for the Rejuvenation of the Great Han Nationality"; "Rejuvenate Han Culture, Amend the History of the Ming Dynasty That Has Been Defamed and Tampered With"; and "Inherit and Promote Traditional Culture of Huaxia."
99. Frazier and Zhang, "Ethnic Identity and Racial Contestation in Cyberspace," 239. Also see Wu, *Chinese Cyber Nationalism*; G. Yang, *Power of the Internet in China*; Y. Zhao, *Communications in China*.
100. Côté, "Political Mobilization of a Regional Minority," 1866.
101. Bovingdon, "The Not-So-Silent Majority"; Prybyla, "Hsia-Fang."
102. Teufel-Dreyer, "Go West Young Han."

103. Sautman, "Ethnic Law and Minority Rights in China."
104. McCarthy, *Communist Multiculturalism*.
105. Bulag, *The Mongols at China's Edge*; Carlson, *Unifying China, Integrating with the World*; Howland, "Dialectics of Chauvinism."
106. An excellent analysis of this tension is I. Johnson, *Souls of China*.
107. Mungello, *Great Encounter*, 21.
108. Mungello, *Great Encounter*, 27.
109. Mungello, *Great Encounter*, 33–36, 53–65.
110. An exceptional analysis of this debate is Y. C. Wang, *Chinese Intellectuals and the West*.
111. On the last example, see Sarotte, "China's Fear of Contagion."
112. Sorman, *Empire of Lies*, 52, 71.
113. Mungello, "Reinterpreting the History of Christianity in China," 538.

4. IMPLICATIONS FOR CHINESE FOREIGN POLICY

1. Leites, *Operational Code of the Politburo*.
2. Friedberg, *A Contest for Supremacy*, 269.
3. Weiss, "Popular Protest, Nationalism, and Domestic-International Linkages in Chinese Politics."
4. See Hudson and Vore, "Foreign Policy Analysis Yesterday, Today, and Tomorrow."
5. H. Liu, "New Migrants and the Revival of Overseas Chinese Nationalism."
6. Reilly, "A Wave to Worry About?"
7. Perry, "Challenging the Mandate of Heaven," 168.
8. D. Zhao, "Nationalism and Authoritarianism."
9. Reilly, *Strong Society, Smart State*.
10. See, for example, Chen, "Nationalism, Internationalism, and Chinese Foreign Policy"; Liew and Wang, *Nationalism, Democracy, and National Integration in China*; and S. Zhao, "Chinese Nationalism and Its International Orientations."
11. Chen, *Social Protests and Contentious Authoritarianism*, 191.
12. You, "Nationalism, the Chinese Defence Culture and the People's Liberation Army," 249.
13. Kaufman, "Escaping the Symbolic Politics Trap."
14. G. Yang, "The Return of Ideology and the Future of Chinese Internet Policy"; S. Zhao, "China's Pragmatic Nationalism."
15. Liu's remarks were posted on www.ncn.org and quoted in Jacques, *When China Rules the World*, 260.
16. McDonald, "China Forgets Manners as Rice Visit Touches Nerves."
17. Jacques, "The Middle Kingdom Mentality."

18. According to Han, "Liberal-leaning users regard their counterparts as violent and irrational extremists whose actions bring shame upon China on the global stage." See Han, *Micro-Blogging Memories*, 120.
19. Christensen, "The Advantage of an Assertive China," 60–61. See also Fewsmith and Rosen, "The Domestic Context of Chinese Foreign Policy."
20. Swaine, "China's Assertive Behavior—Part Three."
21. Chew and Wang, "Online Cultural Conservatism and Han Ethnicism in China."
22. Lampton, "Xi Jinping and the National Security Commission."
23. Mulvenon, "Xi Jinping and the Central Military Commission."
24. You, "The PLA and Diplomacy."
25. Li, "The People's Liberation Army and China's Smart Power Quandary in Southeast Asia"; Scobell, "Is There a Civil-Military Gap in China's Peaceful Rise?"
26. Liu and Ren, "An Emerging Consensus on the U.S. Threat."
27. Page, "For Xi, a 'China Dream' of Military Power."
28. Jakobson, *China's Unpredictable Maritime Security Actors*.
29. You, "The PLA and Diplomacy."
30. Pei, "China's Fragile Mindset." Also see Pei, *China's Crony Capitalism*.
31. Mao was in the Soviet Union from December 1949 through February 1950 to meet with Stalin. On this difficult visit, for both Mao and Stalin, see Chang and Halliday, *Mao: The Unknown Story*, 350–55.
32. Pye, *Spirit of Chinese Politics*, 50, 56.
33. Classics of Chinese strategic thought emphasize the importance of understanding the psychological state of the adversary. Examples may be found in Sun Bin, *Art of Warfare*, and Sun Tzu, *Art of Warfare*. Also see Di Cosmo, *Military Culture in Imperial China*, 1–22, and E. Dreyer, "Continuity and Change," 19–38. For an overview of the impact of Chinese culture, see Johnston, *Cultural Realism*, 22–27.
34. Boodberg, "The Art of War in Ancient China," xix–xx.
35. Paine, *Sino-Japanese War of 1894–1895*, 335.
36. Westad, *Restless Empire*, 31.
37. Sautman, "Myths of Descent, Racial Nationalism, and Ethnic Minorities," 84. Also see Stafford, "The Discourse of Race in Modern China."
38. Previous research has shown that ethnocentrism can contribute to conflict escalation. For example, see Fisher, *Social Psychology of Intergroup and International Conflict Resolution*, and Friend and Thayer, "Evolution and Foreign Policy."
39. Deng's twenty-four-character instruction is quoted in Kissinger, *On China*, 438.
40. Sawyer, *Tao of Spycraft*.
41. Kissinger, *On China*, 30.
42. Waldron, "The Art of *Shi*," 37–39.

43. An excellent analysis of these disputes is Raine and le Mière's *Regional Disorder*.

44. For a review, see van den Berghe, *Ethnic Phenomenon*.

45. Putnam, *Bowling Alone*; and Putnam, Feldstein, and Cohen, *Better Together*.

46. Gillespie, *South-South Transfer*, 168.

47. Crankshaw and Talbott, *Khrushchev Remembers*, 504.

48. Burgman, "China: Embracing Africa but Not Africans."

49. Lan, *Mapping the New Chinese Diaspora in China*, 24, quoting Fennell, "Race," 269.

50. Fennell, "Race," 270–72. Also see Manji and Marks, *African Perspectives on China in Africa*, and Moyo, *Winner Take All*.

51. Brautigam, *Dragon's Gift*, 149.

52. See Alden, Large, and Soares de Oliveira, *China Returns to Africa*; Sharife, "China's New Colonialism"; and Shinn and Eisenman, *China and Africa*.

53. French, *China's Second Continent*.

54. Lumumba-Kasongo, "China-Africa Relations."

55. McGreal, "Thanks China, Now Go Home."

56. McGreal, "Thanks China, Now Go Home."

57. Samora, "Who Is the Bull in a China Shop?"

58. Samora, "Who Is the Bull in a China Shop?"

59. Samora, "Who Is the Bull in a China Shop?"

60. Samora, "Who Is the Bull in a China Shop?" On the impact of cheap Chinese goods, see Taylor, *China's New Role in Africa*, 63–88; Alden, *China in Africa*.

61. Taylor, "China's Oil Diplomacy in Africa."

62. Waldron, *China in Africa*, 6. See also Cheru and Calais, "Countering 'New Imperialisms,'" 221–37; Carmody, *The New Scramble for Africa*, 190–94; and Taylor, *China's New Role in Africa*, 167–69.

63. Pilling and Glover, "China Backs Economic Power with Political Muscle in Africa."

64. Cardenal and Araújo, *China's Silent Army*, 72–74.

65. Murphy, "China Steps Up Push into Latin America."

66. Cardenal and Araújo, *China's Silent Army*, 73–74. Tolerance of corruption is well captured by the remark of Li Puogu, president of the Chinese Exim Bank: "If the water is too clear, you will never catch a fish." Quoted in Cardenal and Araújo, 102.

67. Murphy, "China Steps Up Push into Latin America."

68. Quoted in Cardenal and Araújo, *China's Silent Army*, 143.

69. Cardenal and Araújo, *China's Silent Army*, 110.

70. Cardenal and Araújo, *China's Silent Army*, 110.

71. Cardenal and Araújo, *China's Silent Army*, 260.

5. STRATEGIC ASYMMETRIES FOR THE UNITED STATES

1. The concept of strategic asymmetries has been developed by the Office of Net Assessment in the U.S. Defense Department. In essence, it is the identification of areas of comparative advantage in a competitive relationship. Advantages may be economic, military, political, ideological, or social that produce greater capability, capacity, or efficiency sufficient to change or maintain a balance of power. For a discussion, see Krepinevich and Watts, *Last Warrior*; Marshall, *Long-Term Competition with the Soviets*; Marshall, "The Nature and Scope of Net Assessments," 1; and Skypek, "Evaluating Military Balances through the Lens of Net Assessment."

2. Nye, *Soft Power*, x, 5.

3. Wade, "Time for the West to Practise What It Preaches."

4. Congressional Research Service, *China's Foreign Policy and "Soft Power" in South America, Asia, and Africa.*

5. Consider the efforts to replace English as the language of science. In the summer of 2012, *Quishi Journal* ["求是"杂志], a biweekly publication of the Central Committee of the Chinese Communist Party, whose mission is to spread CCP theories and policies, has called for the creation of an academic language system with Chinese characteristics and style to replace English. The objective is to increase China's soft power by enhancing the affinity, appeal, and influence, as well as to draw scholars throughout the world away from English. See ZH, AF, AT, *Quishi Journal*, June 2012, available at www.qstheory.cn/wz/cmyl/201206/t20120611_163264.htm.

6. Mosher, *China Misperceived.*

7. Lee, *Singapore Story*; Fukuyama, *End of History and the Last Man.*

8. Halper, *Beijing Consensus.*

9. Cole, *China's Quest for Great Power*, 127.

10. BBC, "China Invests $124bn in Belt and Road Global Trade Project." The importance of the AIIB and Belt and Road Initiative are well described in Cole, *China's Quest for Great Power*, and Miller, *China's Asian Dream.*

11. Cole, *China's Quest for Great Power*, 128.

12. French, *Everything under the Heavens*, 257.

13. French, *Everything under the Heavens*, 258.

14. See T. Schwartz, *America's Germany*; Beschloss, *Conquerors*; and Merritt, *Democracy Imposed.*

15. See Halper, *Beijing Consensus.*

16. Yan, *Ancient Chinese Thought, Modern Chinese Power.*

17. Exceptional analyses are Bardhan, *Awakening Giants, Feet of Clay*, and Ogden, *China and India.*

18. Excellent overviews are provided by Di Cosmo, *Ancient China and Its Enemies*; Cosmo, *Military Culture in Imperial China*; and Gordon, *When Asia Was the World*.
19. Jacques, *When China Rules the World*, 392–93.
20. Wang, "Early Ming Relations with Southeast Asia," 61.
21. Wang, "Early Ming Relations with Southeast Asia," 61.
22. Jacques, *When China Rules the World*, 233–71.
23. Synglobe, "Xi Jinping's Five Proposals for the Belt and Road Initiative."
24. Liu, *China Dream*, 100.
25. Quoted in Dikötter, *Imperfect Conceptions*, x. Also see Brooks and Brooks, *Original Analects*, 161.
26. The best critique of eugenics from an evolutionary perspective is Gould, *Mismeasure of Man*. For an account of eugenicist practices in the United States, see Gallagher, *Breeding Better Vermonters*. For an account of eugenicists practices in China, see Chung, "Better Science and Better Race"; Dikötter, *Imperfect Conceptions*; and Sun, *Chinese National Character*.
27. Dikötter, *Imperfect Conceptions*, 1.
28. Dikötter, *Imperfect Conceptions*, 1–2.
29. Quoted in Dikötter, *Imperfect Conceptions*, 160–62.
30. Burger, *Behind the Red Door*, 112. Also see Dikötter, *Sex, Culture, and Modernity in China*.
31. We are grateful to Professor Huiyun Feng for these insights.
32. Mungello, *Great Encounter of China and the West, 1500–1800*, 134–36.
33. On this, see Bardhan, *Awakening Giants, Feet of Clay*.
34. This is the major theme of Lee, *What the U.S. Can Learn from China*.
35. Since 2009, China has overtaken Japan, the EU, and the United States to become ASEAN's largest trading partner.
36. Toh, *Is China an Empire?* 32.
37. Swaine, "Xi Jinping's Trip to Latin America."
38. On China's grab for resources, especially oil, see Carmody, *New Scramble for Africa*, 65–111.
39. See Piccone, "The Geopolitics of China's Rise in Latin America."
40. A good overview is Rachman, *Easternisation*, 212–24. Also see Bickers, *Out of China*.
41. Toh, *Is China an Empire?* 11, 29.
42. Prebisch, *Economic Development of Latin America and Its Principal Problems*.
43. Toh, *Is China an Empire?* 119.
44. This issue is well explored in Ghazvinian, *Untapped*, and Ian Taylor, *China's New Role in Africa*.

45. BBC Chinese, "China's Influence in Africa Continues."
46. Waldron, *China in Africa*, 7.
47. Waldron, *China in Africa*, 7. Also see Rotberg, "China's Quest for Resources, Opportunities, and Influence in Africa."
48. Waldron, *China in Africa*, 7.
49. Toh, *Is China an Empire?* 43, 58–62.
50. Sautman and Yan, "Friends and Interests," 94.
51. Marchal and Desir quoted in Toh, *Is China an Empire?* 57, 61.
52. See Shao, "Go East: African Immigrants in China."
53. U.S. Census Bureau, "Demographic Overview—Custom Region—China," data for 2012.
54. Indeed, a review of their reports reveals nothing on the racist behavior of the Chinese. To their credit, they do address many other human rights abuses by the Chinese, such as freedom of expression.
55. Denyer, "China Urged to Come Clean about 'Grotesque' Level of Capital Punishment." Also see Amnesty International Global Report, *Death Sentences and Executions 2016*.
56. These ideas are expanded in Bechná and Thayer, "NATO's New Role."
57. French, *Everything under the Heavens*, 13–53.
58. Johnson, *Race and Racism in the Chinas*, 128.
59. Gordon G. Chang provides a detailed and thought-provoking analysis of the potential causes of China's collapse in his *Coming Collapse of China*.

6. THE COMING STRUGGLE

1. Kipling, *From Sea to Sea*, 274.
2. See Zhang, *China Wave*.
3. Sorman, *Empire of Lies*, xxvi.
4. Sorman, *Empire of Lies*, xxvi.
5. Quoted in Sorman, *Empire of Lies*, 6.
6. Sorman, *Empire of Lies*, 6–7.

BIBLIOGRAPHY

Agnew, John. "Looking Back to Look Forward: Chinese Geopolitical Narratives and China's Past." *Eurasian Geography and Economics* 53, no. 3 (2012): 301–14.

Ahmed, Akbar S. "'Ethnic Cleansing': A Metaphor for Our Time." *Ethnic and Racial Studies* 18, no. 1 (1995): 1–25.

Alden, Chris. *China in Africa*. London: Zed Books, 2007.

Alden, Chris, Daniel Large, and Ricardo Soares de Oliveira. *China Returns to Africa: A Rising Power and a Continent Embrace*. New York: Columbia University Press, 2008.

Amnesty International Global Report. *Death Sentences and Executions 2016*. London: Amnesty International, 2017.

Anderson, Benedict. *Imagined Communities: Reflections on the Origin and Spread of Nationalism*. Rev. ed. New York: Verso, 1998.

Ashplant, T. G., Graham Dawson, and Michael Roper, eds. *The Politics of War Memory and Commemoration*. New York: Routledge, 2001.

Baidu Tieba. "Inherit and Promote Traditional Culture of Huaxia" [继承和弘扬华夏传统文化]. Available at http://tieba.baidu.com/f?kw=%e5%8d%8e% e5%a4 %8f&frs=yqtb.

———. "Rejuvenate Han and Develop China, Strive for the Rejuvenation of the Great Han Nationality" [興漢振華,為偉大的漢民族復興而努力]. Available at http:// tieba.baidu.com/f?kw=% bb%aa%cf%c4%ba%ba%c3%f1%d7%e5.

———. "Rejuvenate Han Culture, Amend the History of the Ming Dynasty That Has Been Defamed and Tampered With" [复兴汉 文化、修正被诋毁篡改的明朝历史. Available at http://tieba.baidu.com/f?kw=%e6% 98%8e%e6%9c%9d&frs=yqtb.

Balibar, Etienne, and Immanuel Wallerstein. *Race, Nation, and Class: Ambiguous Identities*. London: Verso, 1991.

Baranovitch, Nimrod. "Others No More: The Changing Representations of Non-Han Peoples in Chinese History Textbooks, 1951–2003." *Journal of Asian Studies* 69, no. 1 (2010): 85–122.

Bardhan, Pranab. *Awakening Giants, Feet of Clay: Assessing the Economic Rise of China and India*. Princeton: Princeton University Press, 2010.

Barmé, Geremie R. "To Screw Foreigners Is Patriotic: China's Advent-Garde Nationalist." *China Journal*, no. 34 (July 1995): 209–34.

BBC. "China Invests $124bn in Belt and Road Global Trade Project." May 14, 2017. Available at www.bbc.co.uk/news/world-asia-39912671.

BBC Chinese. "China's Influence in Africa Continues." September 26, 2012. Available at www.bbc.co.uk/zhongwen/simp/chinese_news/2012/09/120926_china _africa.shtml.

Bechná, Zinaida, and Bradley A. Thayer. "NATO's New Role: The Alliance's Response to a Rising China." *Naval War College Review* 69, no. 3 (2016): 65–81.

Bernstein, Richard, and Ross H. Munro. "The Coming Conflict with America." *Foreign Affairs* 76, no. 2 (1997): 18–32.

Berry, Chris. "'Race' [民 族]): Chinese Film and the Politics of Nationalism." *Cinema Journal* 3, no. 2 (1992): 45–58.

Bertrand, Jacques. *Nationalism and Ethnic Conflict in Indonesia*. Cambridge: Cambridge University Press, 2004.

Beschloss, Michael. *The Conquerors: Roosevelt, Truman, and the Destruction of Hitler's Germany, 1941–1945*. New York: Simon and Schuster, 2002.

Bickers, Robert. *Out of China: How the Chinese Ended the Era of Western Domination*. London: Allen Lane/Penguin, 2017.

Bislev, Ane. "Nationalist Netizens in China: Online Historical Memory." *Journal of China and International Relations* 2, no. 1 (2014): 117–36.

Blagojevic, Bojana. "Causes of Ethnic Conflict: A Conceptual Framework." *Journal of Global Change and Governance* 3, no. 1 (2009): 1–25.

Blainey, Geoffrey. *The Causes of Wars*. New York: Free Press, 1973.

Blanchard, Ben, and Antoni Slodkowski. "China Marks 'National Humiliation Day' with Anti-Japanese Protests." *Christian Science Monitor*, September 18, 2012. Available at www.csmonitor.com/World/Latest-News-Wires/2012/0918/China -marks-National-Humiliation-Day-with-anti-Japanese-protests-video.

Bodeen, Christopher. "Beijing Report Says Chinese Muslims Are in Syria." Associated Press, October 29, 2012. Available at http://ratsass.krvw.com/mailman/private /access/attachments/20121029/53013206/attachment.html.

Boodberg, Peter A. "The Art of War in Ancient China: A Study Based upon the *Dialogues of Li Duke of Wei*." PhD diss., University of California, Berkeley, 1930.

Bovingdon, Gardner. *Autonomy in Xinjiang: Han Nationalist Imperatives and Uyghur Discontent.* Washington DC: East-West Center Washington, 2004.

———. "The Not-So-Silent Majority: Uyghur Resistance to Han Rule in Xinjiang." *Modern China* 28, no. 1 (2002): 39–78.

Brautigam, Deborah. *The Dragon's Gift: The Real Story of China in Africa.* New York: Oxford University Press, 2009.

Brooks, E. Bruce, and A. Taeko Brooks, trans. *The Original Analects: Sayings of Confucius and His Successors.* New York: Columbia University Press, 1998.

Broomfield, Emma V. "Perceptions of Danger: The China Threat Theory." *Journal of Contemporary China* 12, no. 35 (2003): 265–84.

Brubaker, Rogers. "Ethnicity, Race, and Nationalism." *Annual Review of Sociology* 35 (2009): 21–42.

Buckley, Chris. "China Warns Officials against 'Dangerous' Western Values." *New York Times*, May 13, 2013. Available at www.nytimes.com/2013/05/14/world/asia/chinese-leaders-warn-of-dangerous-western-values.html.

Bulag, Uradyn E. *The Mongols at China's Edge: History and the Politics of National Unity.* Lanham: Rowman and Littlefield, 2002.

Burger, Richard. *Behind the Red Door: Sex in China.* Hong Kong: Earnshaw Books, 2012.

Burgman, Paul R., Jr. "China: Embracing Africa but Not Africans." *Diplomat*, January 29, 2015. Available at http://thediplomat.com/2015/01/china-embracing-africa-but-not-africans/.

Cairns, E. D., and Micheal D. Roe. "Introduction: Why Memories in Conflict?." In *The Role of Memory in Ethnic Conflict*, edited by Cairns and Roe, 3–8. New York: Palgrave Macmillan, 2003.

Callahan, William A. *China: The Pessoptimist Nation.* Oxford: Oxford University Press, 2010.

———. "National Insecurities: Humiliation, Salvation, and Chinese Nationalism." *Alternatives* 29 (2004): 199–218.

Cardenal, Juan Pablo, and Heriberto Araújo. *China's Silent Army: The Pioneers, Traders, Fixers, and Workers Who Are Remaking the World in Beijing's Image.* Translated by Catherine Mansfield. New York: Crown, 2013.

Carlson, Allen. "A Flawed Perspective: The Limitations Inherent within the Study of Chinese Nationalism." *Nations and Nationalism* 15, no. 1 (2009): 20–35.

———. *Unifying China, Integrating with the World: Securing Chinese Sovereignty in the Reform Area.* Stanford: Stanford University Press, 2002.

Carmody, Pádraig. *The New Scramble for Africa.* Malden MA: Polity Press, 2011.

Carrico, Kevin, and Peter H. Gries. "Nations and Nationalism Roundtable Discussion on Chinese Nationalism and National Identity." *Nations and Nationalisms* 22, no. 3 (2016): 415–46.

"The CCP Central Committee's Notification about Issuing 'The Implementation Outline of Patriotic Education'" [中共中央关于印发《爱国主义教 育实施纲要》 的通知]. *Xinhua Net*, August 8, 1994. Available at http://news.xinhuanet.com /ziliao/ 2005–03/16/content_2705546.htm.

Chang, Gordon G. *The Coming Collapse of China*. London: Random House Business, 2001.

Chang, Jung, and Jon Halliday. *Mao: The Unknown Story*. New York: Knopf, 2005.

Chang, Sidney H., and Leonard H. D. Gordon. *All under Heaven: Sun Yat-sen and His Revolutionary Thought*. Stanford: Hoover Institution Press, 1991.

Chase, Thomas. "Nationalism and the Net: Online Discussion of Goguryeo History in China and South Korea." *China Information* 25, no. 1 (2011): 61–82.

Cheek, Timothy. *The Intellectual in Modern Chinese History*. Cambridge: Cambridge University Press, 2016.

Chen, Jian. *Mao's China and the Cold War*. Chapel Hill: University of North Carolina Press, 2001.

Cheng, Yinghong. "From Campus Racism to Cyber Racism: Discourse of Race and Chinese Nationalism." *China Quarterly* 27 (2011): 561–79.

Cheru, Fantu, and Cyril Obi, eds. *The Rise of China and India in Africa: Challenges, Opportunities, and Critical Interventions*. London: Zed Books, 2010.

Cheru, Fantu, and Magnus Calais. "Countering 'New Imperialism': What Role for the New Partnership for Africa's Development." In *The Rise of China & India in Africa: Challenges, Opportunities, and Critical Interventions*. edited by Cheru and Obi, 221-237. London. Zed Books, 2010.

Chen, Xi. *Social Protests and Contentious Authoritarianism in China*. New York: Cambridge University Press, 2012.

Chen Zhimin. "Nationalism, Internationalism, and Chinese Foreign Policy." *Journal of Contemporary China* 14, no. 42 (2005): 35–53.

Chew, Matthew M., and Yi Wang. "Online Cultural Conservatism and Han Ethnicism in China." *Asian Social Sciences* 8, no. 7 (2012): 3–10.

Chow, Kai-wing. "Imagining Boundaries of Blood: Zhang Binglin and the Invention of the Chinese Race in Modern China." In *The Construction of Racial Identities in China and Japan: Historical and Contemporary Perspectives*, edited by Frank Dikötter, 34–52. Honolulu: University of Hawaii Press, 1997.

———. "Narrating Nation, Race, and National Culture: Imagining the Hanzu Identity in Modern China." In *Constructing Nationhood in Modern East Asia*, edited by Kai-wing Chow, Kevin M. Doak, and Poshek Fu, 47–84. Ann Arbor: University of Michigan Press, 2001.

Christensen, Thomas J. "The Advantage of an Assertive China: Responding to Beijing's Abrasive Diplomacy." *Foreign Affairs* 90, no. 2 (2011): 54–67.

Christiansen, Thomas. "A Liberal Institutionalist Perspective on China-EU Relations." In *China, the European Union, and the International Politics of Global Governance*, edited by Jianwei Wang and Weiqing Song, 29–50. London: Palgrave Macmillan, 2016.

Chu, Yiting. "The Power of Knowledge: A Critical Analysis of the Depiction of Ethnic Minorities in China's Elementary Textbooks." *Journal of Race, Ethnicity, and Education* 18, no. 4 (2015): 469–87.

Chung, Yuehtsen Juliette. "Better Science and Better Race: Social Darwinism and Chinese Eugenics." *Isis* 105, no. 4 (2014): 793–802.

Cohen, Paul A. *Speaking to History: The Story of King Goujian in Twentieth-Century China*. Berkeley: University of California Press, 2009.

Cole, Bernard D. *China's Quest for Great Power: Ships, Oil, and Foreign Policy*. Annapolis: Naval Institute Press, 2016.

Congressional Research Service. *China's Foreign Policy and "Soft Power" in South America, Asia, and Africa*. Washington DC: Government Printing Office, 2008.

Costa, Anna. "Focusing on Chinese Nationalism: An Inherently Flawed Perspective? A Reply to Allen Carlson." *Nations and Nationalism* 20, no. 1 (2014): 93–112.

Côté, Isabelle. "Political Mobilization of a Regional Minority: Han Chinese Settlers in Xinjiang." *Ethnic and Racial Studies* 34, no. 11 (2011): 1855–73.

Crankshaw, Edward, and Strobe Talbott, *Khrushchev Remembers*. Boston: Little, Brown, 1970.

Denyer, Simon. "China Urged to Come Clean about 'Grotesque' Level of Capital Punishment." *Washington Post*, April 10, 2017. Available at www.washingtonpost.com/news/worldviews/wp/2017/04/10/china-urged-to-come-clean-about-grotesque-level-of-capital-punishment/.

Di Cosmo, Nicola. *Ancient China and Its Enemies: The Rise of Nomadic Power in East Asian History*. New York: Cambridge University Press, 2002.

———. *Military Culture in Imperial China*. Cambridge: Harvard University Press, 2009.

Dikötter, Frank. *The Discourse of Race in Modern China*. Stanford: Stanford University Press, 1992.

———. *The Discourse of Race in Modern China*. 2nd ed. Oxford: Oxford University Press, 2015.

———. *Imperfect Conceptions: Medical Knowledge, Birth Defects, and Eugenics in China*. New York: Columbia University Press, 1998.

———. "Racial Identity in China: Context and Meaning." *China Quarterly* 138 (1994): 404–12.

———. *Sex, Culture, and Modernity in China: Medical Science and the Construction of Sexual Identities in the Early Republican Period*. Honolulu: University of Hawai'i Press, 1997.

————, ed. *The Construction of Racial Identities in China and Japan*. Honolulu: University of Hawai'i Press, 1997.

Dreyer, Edward L. "Continuity and Change." In *A Military History of China*, edited by David A. Graff and Robin Higham, 19–38. Boulder: Westview Press, 2002.

Dreyer, June T. *China's Forty Millions: Minority Nationalities and National Integration in the People's Republic of China*. Cambridge: Harvard University Press, 1976.

Duara, Prasenjit. *Culture, Power, and the State: Rural North China, 1900–1942*. Stanford: Stanford University Press, 1988.

————. "De-constructing the Chinese Nation." *Australian Journal of Chinese Affairs* 30 (1993): 1–26.

————. *Rescuing History from the Nation: Questioning Narratives of Modern China*. Chicago: University of Chicago Press, 1995.

Economy, Elizabeth C. "China's Imperial President: Xi Jinping Tightens His Grip." *Foreign Affairs* 93, no. 6 (2014): 80–93.

Edwards, Louise. "Narratives of Race and Nation in China: Women's Suffrage in the Early Twentieth Century." *Women's Studies International Forum* 25, no. 6 (2002): 619–30.

Eller, Jack David. *From Culture to Ethnicity to Conflict: An Anthropological Perspective on Ethnic Conflict*. Ann Arbor: University of Michigan Press, 1999.

Elliott, Mark C. *The Manchu Way: The Eight Banners and Ethnic Identity in Late Imperial China*. Stanford: Stanford University Press, 2001.

Fairbank, John K. "Tributary Trade and China's Relations with the West." *Far Eastern Quarterly* 1, no. 2 (1943): 129–49.

————, ed., *The Chinese World Order: Traditional China's Foreign Relations*. Cambridge: Harvard University Press, 1968.

Feng, Chongyi. "Nationalism and Democratisation in Contemporary China." *Global Dialogue* 9, nos. 1–2 (2007): 49–59.

Fennell, Vera Leigh. "Race: China's Question and Problem." *Review of Black Political Economy* 40, no. 3 (2013): 245–75.

Fewsmith, Joseph, and Stanley Rosen. "The Domestic Context of Chinese Foreign Policy: Does Public Opinion Matter?" In *The Making of Chinese Foreign and Security Policy in the Era of Reform*, edited by David Lampton, 151–90. Stanford: Stanford University Press, 2001.

Fisher, Ronald J. *The Social Psychology of Intergroup and International Conflict Resolution*. New York: Springer, 1990.

Fiskesjö, Magnus. "Rescuing the Empire: Chinese Nation-Building in the Twentieth Century." *European Journal of East Asian Studies* 5, no. 1 (2006): 15–44.

Fitzgerald, John. "The Nationless State: The Search for a Nation in Modern Chinese Nationalism." *Australian Journal of Chinese Affairs*, no. 33 (1995): 75–104.

Fravel, M. Taylor. *Strong Borders, Secure Nation: Cooperation and Conflict in China's Territorial Disputes*. Princeton: Princeton University Press, 2008.

Frazier, Robeson Taj, and Lin Zhang. "Ethnic Identity and Racial Contestation in Cyberspace: Deconstructing the Chineseness of Lou Jing." *China Information* 28, no. 2 (2014): 237–58.

French, Howard W. *China's Second Continent: How a Million Migrants Are Building a New Empire in Africa*. New York: Vintage, 2015.

———. *Everything under the Heavens: How the Past Helps Shape China's Push for Global Power*. London: Scribe, 2017.

Friedberg, Aaron L. *A Contest for Supremacy: China, America, and the Struggle for Mastery in Asia*. New York: Norton, 2011.

Friedman, Edward. "Raising Sheep on Wolf Milk: The Politics and Dangers of Mis-remembering the Past in China." *Totalitarian Movements and Political Religions* 9, no. 2–3 (2008): 389–409.

Friedrichs, Jörg. "Sino-Muslim Relations: The Han, the Hui, and the Uyghurs." *Journal of Muslim Minority Affairs* 37, no. 1 (2017): 55–79.

Friend, John M., and Bradley A. Thayer. "Evolution and Foreign Policy: Insights for Decision-Making Models." In *Biopolicy: The Life Sciences and Public Policy*, edited by Albert Somit and Steven A. Peterson, 97–117. Bingley, UK: Emerald, 2012.

Fukuyama, Francis. *The End of History and the Last Man*. New York: Free Press, 1992.

Gagnon, V. P., Jr. "Ethnic Nationalism and International Conflict: The Case of Serbia." *International Security* 19, no. 3 (1994–95): 130–66.

Gallagher, Nancy L. *Breeding Better Vermonters: The Eugenics Project in the Green Mountain State*. Hanover NH: University Press of New England, 1999.

Ghazvinian, John. *Untapped: The Scramble for Africa's Oil*. New York: Harcourt, 2007.

Gillespie, Sandra. *South-South Transfer: A Study of Sino-African Exchanges*. New York: Routledge, 2001.

Gilley, Bruce. *Tiger on the Brink: Jiang Zemin and China's New Elite*. Berkeley: University of California Press, 1998.

Gladney, Dru C. *Dislocating China: Reflections on Muslims, Minorities, and Other Subaltern Subjects*. London: Hurst, 2004.

Glaser, Charles. "Will China's Rise Lead to War? Why Realism Does Not Mean Pessimism." *Foreign Affairs* 90, no. 2 (2011): 80–91.

Gonzalez-Vicente, Ruben. "The Empire Strikes Back? China's New Racial Sovereignty." *Political Geography* 59 (2017): 139–41.

Gordon, Stewart. *When Asia Was the World*. Philadelphia: Da Capo Press, 2008.

Gould, Stephen Jay. *The Mismeasure of Man*. Rev. ed. New York: Norton, 1996.

Gries, Peter Hays. *China's New Nationalism: Pride, Politics, and Diplomacy*. Berkeley: University of California Press, 2004.

———. "Chinese Nationalism: Challenging the State." *Current History* 104, no. 683 (2005): 251–56.

———. "The Koguryo Controversy, National Identity, and Sino-Korean Relations Today." *East Asia* 22, no. 4 (2005): 3–17.

Gries, Peter Hays, Derek Steiger, and Tao Wang. "Popular Nationalism and China's Japan Policy: The Diaoyu Islands Protests, 2012–2013." *Journal of Contemporary China* 25, no. 98 (2016): 264–76.

Guo, Jinyue. "The Different Images of Putin between China and the United States and the Implications" [普京在中美两国的不同形象及启. *International Communication* [对外传播] 4 (2014): 12–14.

Guo, Yinggjie. "Patriotic Villains and Patriotic Heroes: Chinese Literary Nationalism in the 1990s." *Nationalism and Ethnic Politics* 4, no. 1–2 (1998): 163–88.

Hagan, Joe D. "Domestic Political Systems and War Proneness." *Mershon International Studies Review* 38, no. 2 (1994): 183–207.

Halbwachs, Maurice. *On Collective Memory.* Translated by Lewis A. Coser. Chicago: University of Chicago Press, 1992.

Hall, Stuart. "The Question of Cultural Identity." In *Modernity and Its Futures: Understanding Modern Societies, Book IV,* edited by Stuart Hall, David Held, and Tony McGrew, 273–326. Cambridge: Polity Press, 1992.

Halper, Stefan. *The Beijing Consensus: How China's Authoritarian Model Will Dominate the Twenty-first Century.* New York: Basic Books, 2010.

Han, Eileen L. *Micro-Blogging Memories: Weibo and Collective Remembering in Contemporary China.* New York: Palgrave Macmillan, 2016.

Han, Enze. "Boundaries, Discrimination, and Interethnic Conflict in Xinjiang, China." *International Journal of Conflict and Violence* 4, no. 2 (2010): 244–56.

Harris, Peter. "Chinese Nationalism: The State and the Nation." *China Journal*, no. 38 (1997): 121–37.

Harrison, Henrietta. *The Making of the Republican Citizen: Political Ceremonies and Symbols in China, 1911–1929.* Oxford: Oxford University Press, 2000.

Hasmath, Reza. "The Interactions of Ethnic Minorities in Beijing." Working Paper no. 14–111, Oxford University, Centre on Migration, Policy and Society, 2014.

He, Kai. *China's Crisis Behavior: Political Survival and Foreign Policy after the Cold War.* Cambridge: Cambridge University Press, 2016.

Heberer, Thomas. *China and Its National Minorities.* Armonk NY: M. E. Sharpe, 1989.

Hevi, Emmanuel John. *An African Student in China.* New York: Praeger, 1963.

Holbig, Heike, and Bruce Gilley. "Reclaiming Legitimacy in China." *Politics & Policy* 38, no. 3 (2010): 395–422.

Hood, Johanna. "Distancing Disease in the Un-Black Han Chinese Politic: Othering Difference in China's HIV/AIDS Media." *Modern China* 39, no. 3 (2013): 280–318.

Horesh, Niv, Hyun Jin Kim, Peter Mauch, and Jonathan Sullivan. "Is My Rival's Rival a Friend? Popular Third-Party Perceptions of Territorial Disputes in East Asia." *Copenhagen Journal of Asian Studies* 32, no. 1 (2014): 5–25.

Horowitz, Donald. *Ethnic Groups in Conflict.* Berkeley: University of California Press, 1985.

Howland, Douglas. "The Dialectics of Chauvinism: Minority Nationalities and Territorial Sovereignty in Mao Zedongs' New Democracy." *Modern China* 37, no. 2 (2011): 170–201.

Hudson, Valerie, and Christopher S. Vore. "Foreign Policy Analysis Yesterday, Today, and Tomorrow." *Mershon International Studies Review* 39, no. 2 (1995): 209–38.

Hughes, Christopher R. "Nationalism and Multilateralism in Chinese Foreign Policy: Implications for Southeast Asia." *Pacific Review* 18, no. 1 (2005): 119–35.

———. "Reclassifying Chinese Nationalism: The Geopolitik Turn." *Journal of Contemporary China* 20, no. 71 (2011): 601–20.

Hutchinson, John. *Nationalism and War.* Oxford: Oxford University Press, 2017.

Hyer, Eric. "China's Policy towards Uighur Nationalism." *Journal of Muslim Minority Affairs* 26, no. 1 (2006): 75–86.

———. "Sinocentricism and the National Question in China." In *Nations and Their Histories: Constructions and Representations,* edited by Susana Carvalho and François Gemenne, 255–73. New York: Palgrave Macmillan, 2009.

Ikenberry, G. John. "The Rise of China and the Future of the West: Can the Liberal System Survive?" *Foreign Affairs* 87, no. 1 (2008): 23–37.

"Inherit the Past, Usher in the Future, Continue to Press Forward to the Goal of Chinese Nation's Great Rejuvenation" [习近平: 承前启后 继往开来 继续朝着中华民族伟大复兴目标奋勇前进]. *Xinhua Net,* November 11, 2012. Available at http://news.xinhuanet.com/politics/2012–11/29/c_113852724.htm.

Irwin, Peter. "Why Is China Banning Baby Names and Beards in Xinjiang?" *Diplomat,* April 29, 2017. Available at http://thediplomat.com/2017/04/why-is-china -banning-baby-names- and-beards-in-xinjiang/.

Jacobs, Andrew. "Xinjiang Seethes under Chinese Crackdown." *New York Times,* January 2, 2016. Available at www.nytimes.com/2016/01/03/world/asia/xinjiang -seethes-under-chinese-crackdown.html.

Jacques, Martin. "The Middle Kingdom Mentality: At Last China's Culture of Racism is Being Contested by Chinese." *Guardian,* April 16, 2005, 24.

———. *When China Rules the World: The End of the Western World and the Birth of a New Global Order.* New York: Penguin Press, 2009..

Jakobson, Linda. *China's Unpredictable Maritime Security Actors.* Lowy Institute, December 2014, available at www.lowyinstitute.org/.

Jia Qingguo. "Disrespect and Distrust: The External Origins of Contemporary Chinese Nationalism." *Journal of Contemporary China* 14, no. 42 (2005): 11–21.

Johnson, Ian. *The Souls of China: The Return of Religion after Mao.* New York: Pantheon, 2017.

Johnson, M. Dujon. *Race and Racism in the Chinas.* Bloomington IN: AuthorHouse, 2011.

Johnston, Alastair Iain. *Cultural Realism: Strategic Culture and Grand Strategy in Chinese History.* Princeton: Princeton University Press, 1995.

———. "How New and Assertive Is China's New Assertiveness?" *International Security* 37, no. 4 (2013): 7–48.

———. "Is China a Status Quo Power?" *International Security* 27, no. 4 (2003): 5–56.

———. "Is Chinese Nationalism Rising? Evidence from Beijing." *International Security* 41, no. 3 (2016–17): 7–43.

Joniak-Lüthi, Agnieszka, *The Han: China's Diverse Minority.* Seattle: University of Washington Press, 2015.

Kaltman, Blaine. *Under the Heel of the Dragon: Islam, Racism, Crime, and Uighur in China.* Columbus: Ohio University Press, 2007.

Karl, Rebecca E. *Staging the World: Chinese Nationalism at the Turn of the Twentieth Century.* Durham NC: Duke University Press, 2002.

Kaufman, Alison. "Xi Jinping as Historian: Marxist, Chinese, Nationalist, Global." *Asian Forum,* October 15, 2015. Available at www.theasanforum.org/xi-jinping-as-historian-marxist-chinese-nationalist-global/.

Kaufman, Stuart J. "An 'International' Theory of Inter-Ethnic War." *Review of International Studies* 22, no. 2 (1996): 149–71.

———. "Escaping the Symbolic Politics Trap: Reconciliation Initiatives and Conflict Resolution in Ethnic Wars." *Journal of Peace Research* 43, no. 2 (2006): 201–18.

Keevak, Michael. *Becoming Yellow: A Short History of Racial Thinking.* Princeton: Princeton University Press, 2011.

Kipling, Rudyard. *From Sea to Sea: Letters of Travel.* New York: Doubleday, Page, 1907.

Kipnis, Andrew. "Suzhi: A Key Word Approach." *China Quarterly,* no. 186 (2006): 295–313.

Kissinger, Henry. *On China.* New York: Penguin Books, 2011.

Kowner, Rotem, and Walter Demel. "Modern East Asia and the Rise of Racial Thought: Possible Links, Unique Features, and Unsettled Issues." In *Race and Racism in Modern East Asia: Western and Eastern Constructions,* edited by Rotem Kowner and Walter Demel, 1–37. Leiden: Brill, 2013.

Krepinevich, Andrew, and Barry Watts. *The Last Warrior: Andrew Marshall and the Shaping of American Defense Strategy.* New York: Basic, 2015.

Kuhn, Dieter. *The Age of Confucian Rule: The Song Transformation of China*. Cambridge: Harvard University Press, 2009.

Lai, Ming-yan. *Nativism and Modernity: Cultural Contestations in China and Taiwan under Global Capitalism*. Albany: State University of New York Press, 2008.

Laitinen, Kauko. *Chinese Nationalism in the Late Qing Dynasty: Zhang Binglin as an Anti-Manchu Propagandist*. London: Curzon Press, 1990.

Lampton, David M. "Xi Jinping and the National Security Commission: Policy Coordination and Political Power." *Journal of Contemporary China* 24, no. 95 (2015): 760–61.

Lan, Shanshan. *Mapping the New Chinese Diaspora in China: Race and the Cultural Politics of Belonging*. New York: Routledge, 2017.

Lee, Ann, *What the U.S. Can Learn from China: An Open-Minded Guide to Treating Our Greatest Competitor as Our Greatest Teacher*. San Francisco: BK Currents, 2012.

Lee Kuan Yew. *The Singapore Story: Memoirs of Lee Kuan Yew*. Singapore: Prentice-Hall, 1998.

Leibold, James. "Competing Narratives of Racial Unity in Republican China: From the Yellow Emperor to Peking Man." *Modern China* 32, no. 2 (2006): 181–220.

———. "Han Cybernationalism and State Territorialization in the People's Republic of China." *China Information* 30, no. 1 (2016): 3–28.

———. "More than a Category: Han Supremacism on the Chinese Internet." *China Quarterly* 203 (2010): 539–59.

———. "Xinhai Remembered: From Han Racial Revolution to Revival of the Chinese Nation." *Asian Ethnicity* 15, no. 1 (2014): 1–20.

Leites, Nathan. *The Operational Code of the Politburo*. Santa Monica: RAND, 1951.

Lemos, Gerard. *The End of the Chinese Dream: Why Chinese People Fear the Future*. New Haven: Yale University Press, 2012.

Lenin, Vladimir. *Imperialism: The Highest Stage of Capitalism*. Moscow: Progress, 1982.

Levin, Dan. "China Tells Schools to Suppress Western Ideas, with One Big Exception." *New York Times*, February 9, 2015. Available at www.nytimes. com/2015 /02/10/world/asia/china-tells-schools- to-suppress-western-ideas-with-one-big -exception.html.

Li, Mingjiang. "The People's Liberation Army and China's Smart Power Quandary in Southeast Asia." *Journal of Strategic Studies* 38, no. 2 (2015): 359–82.

Li Weihan. "Guanyu Minzu gongzuozhong de jige wenti" [On some questions encountered in the nationality work, September 1961]. In *Li Weihan Xuanji* [Selected works of Li Weihan]. Beijing: Renmin Chubanshe, 1987.

Liew, Leong H., and Shaoguang Wang, eds. *Nationalism, Democracy, and National Integration in China*. New York: Routledge, 2004.

Lilley, James R. "Nationalism Bites Back." *New York Times*, October 24, 1996, A27.

Lin, Jing. "Policies and Practices of Bilingual Education for the Minorities in China." *Journal of Multilingual and Multicultural Development* 18, no. 3 (1997): 193–205.

Link, Perry. "China's 'Core' Problem: Ideology." *Daedalus* 122, no. 2 (1993): 189–205.

Liu, Hong. "New Migrants and the Revival of Overseas Chinese Nationalism." *Journal of Contemporary China* 14, no. 43 (2005): 291–316.

Liu Mingfu. *The China Dream*. New York: CN Times Books, 2015.

Liu, Shih-Diing. "China's Popular Nationalism on the Internet: Report on the 2005 Anti-Japanese Network Struggles." *Inter-Asia Cultural Studies* 7, no. 2 (2006): 144–55.

Liu Xiaobo. *No Enemies, No Hatred: Selected Essays and Poems*. Cambridge: Belknap, 2012.

Liu, Yawei, and Justine Zheng Ren. "An Emerging Consensus on the U.S. Threat: The United States according to PLA Officers." *Journal of Contemporary China* 23, no. 86 (2013): 255–75.

Lumumba-Kasongo, Tukumbi. "China-Africa Relations: A Neo-Imperialism or a Neo-Colonialism: A Reflection." *African and Asian Studies* 10 (2011): 234–66.

Mancall, Mark. "The Ch'ing Tribute System: An Interpretative Essay." In *The Chinese World Order: Traditional China's Foreign Relations*, edited by John K. Fairbank, 63–89. Cambridge: Harvard University Press, 1968.

Manji, Firoze, and Stephen Marks, eds. *African Perspectives on China in Africa*. Oxford: Fahamu, 2007.

Mao Tsetung. "Pipan da Hanzu Zhuyi [Inner-Party Directive Drafted for the Central Committee of the CCP, March 16, 1953]." In *Selected Readings of Mao Tsetung*, vol. 5. Peking: Foreign Languages, 1971.

Marriott, David, and Karl Lacroix. *Fault Lines on the Face of China: 50 Reasons Why China May Never Be Great*. N.P.: CreateSpace Independent Publishing Platform, 2010.

Marshall, Andrew W. *Long-Term Competition with the Soviets: A Framework for Strategic Analysis*. Santa Monica: RAND, 1972.

———. "The Nature and Scope of Net Assessments." NSC memorandum, August 16, 1972.

McCarthy, Susan K. *Communist Multiculturalism: Ethnic Revival in Southwest China*. Seattle: University of Washington Press, 2009.

McDonald, Hamish. "China Forgets Manners as Rice Visit Touches Nerves." *Sydney Morning Post*, March 26, 2005. Available at www.smh.com.au/articles/2005/03/25/1111692629223.html?from=top5&oneclick=true.

McGreal, Chris. "Thanks China, Now Go Home: Buy-Up of Zambia Revives Old Colonial Fears." *Guardian*, 5 February 2007. Available at www.guardian.co.uk/world/2007/feb/05/china.chrismcgreal.

Merritt, Richard L. *Democracy Imposed: U.S. Occupation Policy and the German Public, 1945–1949*. New Haven: Yale University Press, 1995.

Miller, Tom. *China's Asian Dream: Empire Building along the New Silk Road*. London: Zed, 2017.

Mishar, Pankaj. *From the Ruins of Empire: The Intellectuals Who Remade Asia*. New York: Farrar, Straus and Giroux, 2012.

Mosher, Steven W. *China Misperceived: American Illusions and Chinese Reality*. New York: Basic Books, 1990.

Moyo, Dambisa F. *Winner Take All: China's Race for Resources and What It Means for the World*. New York: Basic Books, 2012.

Mulvenon, James. "Xi Jinping and the Central Military Commission: Bridesmaid or Bride?" *China Leadership Monitor* 34 (2011): 1–5.

Mungello, D. E. *The Great Encounter of China and the West, 1500–1800*. 3rd ed. Lanham: Rowman and Littlefield, 2009.

———. "Reinterpreting the History of Christianity in China." *Historical Journal* 55, no. 2 (2012): 533–52.

Murphy, Colum. "China Steps Up Push into Latin America." *Wall Street Journal*, September 12, 2012. Available at http://online.wsj.com/article/sb1000087239 6390443696604577647102203290514.html.

Nye, Joseph S., Jr. *Soft Power: The Means to Success in World Politics*. New York: Public Affairs, 2004.

Ogden, Chris. *China and India: Asia's Emerging Great Powers*. Malden MA: Polity, 2017.

Page, Jeremy. "For Xi, a 'China Dream' of Military Power." *Wall Street Journal*, March 13, 2013, A1.

Paine, S.C.M. *The Sino-Japanese War of 1894–1895: Perceptions, Power, and Primacy*. New York: Cambridge University Press, 2003.

———. *The Wars for Asia, 1911–1949*. New York: Cambridge University Press, 2012.

Pan, Philip P. *Out of Mao's Shadow: The Struggle for the Soul of a New China*. New York: Simon and Schuster, 2008.

Parker, Andrew, Mary Russo, Doris Sommers, and Patricia Yaeger. Introduction to *Nationalisms and Sexualities*, edited by Parker et al., 1–20. New York: Routledge, 1991.

Patent, Jason D. "China." In *Building Bridges among the BRICs*, edited by Robert Crane, 154–92. New York: Palgrave Macmillan, 2015.

Pei, Minxin. *China's Crony Capitalism: The Dynamics of Regime Decay*. Cambridge: Harvard University Press, 2016.

———. "China's Fragile Mindset." *Christian Science Monitor*, April 9, 2001. Available at www.csmonitor.com/2001/0409/p11s2.html.

People's Republic of China, Ministry of Education. *Teaching Guideline for History Education* [史教学大纲]. Beijing: People's Education Press, 2002.

Perry, Elizabeth. "Challenging the Mandate of Heaven: Popular Protest in Modern China." *Critical Asian Studies* 33, no. 2 (2001): 163–80.

Peterson, Roger D. *Understanding Ethnic Violence: Fear, Hatred, and Resentment in Twentieth-Century Eastern Europe.* Cambridge: Cambridge University Press, 2002.

Piccone, Ted. "The Geopolitics of China's Rise in Latin America." Geoeconomics and Global Issues, Paper 2, Brookings Institution, November 2016. Available at www.brookings.edu/wp-content/uploads/2016/11/the-geopolitics-of-chinas-rise -in-latin-america_ted-piccone.pdf.

Pillemer, David B. "Can the Psychology of Memory Enrich Historical Analyses of Trauma?" *History and Memory* 16, no. 2 (2004): 140–54.

Pilling, David, and Charles Glover. "China Backs Economic Power with Political Muscle in Africa." *Financial Times*, July 12, 2017, 6.

Pillsbury, Michael. *The Hundred-Year Marathon: China's Secret Strategy to Replace America as the Global Superpower.* New York: Henry Holt, 2015.

Pines, Yuri. *The Everlasting Empire: The Political Culture of Ancient China and Its Imperial Legacy.* Princeton: Princeton University Press, 2012.

Prebisch, Raúl. *The Economic Development of Latin America and Its Principal Problems.* New York: United Nations Department of Economic Affairs, 1950.

Prybyla, Jan S. "Hsia-Fang: The Economic and Politics of Rustication in China." *Pacific Affairs* 48, no. 2 (1975): 153–72.

Pusey, James. *China and Charles Darwin.* Cambridge: Council on East Asian Studies, Harvard University, 1983.

Putnam, Robert D. *Bowling Alone: The Collapse and Revival of American Community.* New York: Simon and Schuster, 2001.

Putnam, Robert D., Lewis Feldstein, and Donald J. Cohen. *Better Together: Restoring the American Community.* New York: Simon and Schuster, 2004.

Pye, Lucien. *The Spirit of Chinese Politics.* Cambridge: Harvard University Press, 1992.

Rachman, Gideon. *Easternisation: War and Peace in the Asian Century.* London: Bodley Head, 2016.

Raine, Sarah, and Christian le Mière. *Regional Disorder: The South China Sea Disputes.* New York: Routledge, 2013.

Rauhala, Emily, and Simon Denyer. "Chinese State Media Melt Down over South China Sea Ruling." *Washington Post*, July 12, 2016. Available at www.washingtonpost .com/news/worldviews/wp/2016/07/12/chinese-state-media-melt-down-over -south-china-sea-ruling/.

Rawski, Evelyn S. "Presidential Address: Reenvisioning the Qing: The Significance of the Qing Period in Chinese History." *Journal of Asian Studies* 55, no. 4 (1996): 828–50.

Reilly, James. *Strong Society, Smart State: The Rise of Public Opinion in China's Japan Policy*. New York: Columbia University Press, 2012.

―――. "A Wave to Worry About? Public Opinion, Foreign Policy, and China's Anti-Japan Protest." *Journal of Contemporary China* 23, no. 86 (2014): 197–215.

Rennie, Namvula. "The Lion and the Dragon: African Experiences in China." *Journal of African Media Studies* 1, no. 3 (2009): 379–414.

Rhoads, Edward J. M. *Manchus and Han: Ethnic Relations and Political Power in Late Qing and Early Republican China, 1861–1928*. Seattle: University of Washington Press, 2000.

Ross, Robert S. "Assessing the China Threat." *National Interest* 81 (Fall 2005): 81–87.

Rossabi, Morris. *Governing China's Multiethnic Frontiers*, edited by Rossabi, 3–18. Seattle: University of Washington Press, 2004.

Rotberg, Robert I., ed. *China into Africa: Trade, Aid, and Influence*. Washington DC: Brookings Institution Press, 2008.

Roy, Denny. "The 'China Threat' Issue: Major Arguments." *Asian Survey* 36, no. 8 (1996): 758–71.

Rozman, Gilbert. "Chinese National Identity: A Six-Dimensional Analysis." In *East Asian National Identities: Common Roots and Chinese Exceptionalism*, edited by Gilbert Rozman, 73–100. Stanford: Stanford University Press, 2012.

Sahdra, Baljinder, and Michael Ross. "Group Identification and Historical Memory." *Personality and Social Psychology Bulletin* 33, no. 3 (2007): 384–95.

Saito, Hiro. *The History Problem: The Politics of War Commemoration in East Asia*. Honolulu: University of Hawaii Press, 2016.

Samora, Mwaura. "Who Is the Bull in a China Shop?" *Daily Nation*, August 20, 2012. Available at www.nation.co.ke/Features/dn2/Enter+the+dragon/-/957860 /1483234/-/ejcb57/-/index.html.

Samson, Jane. *Race and Empire*. New York: Pearson Longman, 2005.

Sarotte, M. E. "China's Fear of Contagion: Tiananmen Square and the Power of the European Example." *International Security* 37, no. 2 (2012): 156–82.

Sautman, Barry. "Anti-Black Racism in Post-Mao China." *China Quarterly* 138 (1994): 413–37.

―――. "Ethnic Law and Minority Rights in China: Progress and Constraints." *Law & Policy* 21, no. 3 (1999): 283–314.

―――. "Myths of Descent, Racial Nationalism, and Ethnic Minorities." In *The Construction of Racial Identities in China and Japan*, edited by Frank Dikötter, 75–95. Honolulu: University of Hawai'i Press, 1997.

―――. "Racial Nationalism and China's External Behavior." *World Affairs* 160, no. 2 (1997): 78–95.

Sautman, Barry, and Hairong Yan. "Friends and Interests: China's Distinctive Links with Africa." *African Studies Review* 50, no. 3 (2007): 75–114.

Sawyer, Ralph D. *The Tao of Spycraft: Intelligence Theory and Practice in Traditional China.* Boulder: Westview Press, 1998.

Schell, Orville, and John Delury. *Wealth and Power: China's Long March to the Twenty-First Century.* New York: Random House, 2013.

Schram, Stuart R. *The Political Thought of Mao Tse-tung.* New York: Praeger, 1969.

Schwartz, Benjamin. *In Search of Wealth and Power: Yen Fu and the West.* Cambridge: Harvard University Press, 1964.

Schwartz, Thomas Alan. *America's Germany: John J. McCloy and the Federal Republic of Germany.* Cambridge: Harvard University Press, 1991.

Scobell, Andrew. "Is There a Civil-Military Gap in China's Peaceful Rise?" *Parameters* 39, no. 2 (2009): 4–22.

Seckington, Ian. "Nationalism, Ideology, and China's 'Fourth Generation' Leadership." *Journal of Contemporary China* 14, no. 42 (2005): 23–33.

"Settlers in Xinjiang: Circling the Wagons." *Economist* 407, no. 8837 (May 25, 2013): 45–46.

Shambaugh, David. *China Goes Global: The Partial Power.* New York: Oxford University Press, 2013.

Shao, Kaiyu. "Go East: African Immigrants in China." *Consultancy Africa Intelligence*, March 2, 2012. Available at www.consultancyafrica.com/index.php?option=com _content&view=article&id=963:go-east-african-immigrants-in-china&catid= 58:asia-dimension-discussion-papers&Itemid=264.

Sharife, Khadij. "China's New Colonialism." *Foreign Policy*, September 25, 2009. Available at www.foreignpolicy.com/articles/2009/09/25/chinas_new_colonialism ?page=0,0.

Shen, Simon. "Nationalism or Nationalist Foreign Policy? Contemporary Chinese Nationalism and Its Role in Shaping Chinese Foreign Policy in Response to the Belgrade Embassy Bombing." *Politics* 24, no. 2 (2004): 122–30.

Shen, Simon, and Shaun Breslin, eds. *Online Chinese Nationalism and China's Bilateral Relations.* Lanham: Lexington Books, 2010.

Shen Sung-Chiao. "Discourse on Guomin ('the Citizen') in Late Qing China, 1895–1911." *Inter-Asia Cultural Studies* 7, no. 1 (2006): 2–23.

Shinn, David H., and Joshua Eisenman. *China and Africa: A Century of Engagement.* Philadelphia: University of Pennsylvania Press, 2012.

Shirk, Susan. *China: Fragile Superpower.* Oxford: Oxford University Press, 2007.

Skypek, Thomas. "Evaluating Military Balances through the Lens of Net Assessment: History and Application." *Journal of Military and Strategic Studies* 12, no. 2 (2010): 1–25.

Smith, Anthony. *Ethno-Symbolism and Nationalism: A Cultural Approach.* New York: Routledge, 2009.

———. *National Identity.* Reprint, Reno: University of Nevada Press, 1993.

Smith, Graeme. "Chinese Reactions to Anti-Asian Riots in the Pacific." *Journal of Pacific History* 47, no. 1 (2012): 93–109.

Sneider, Daniel. "Textbooks and Patriotic Education: Wartime Memory Formation in China and Japan." *Asia-Pacific Review* 20, no. 1 (2013): 35–54.

Sorman, Guy. *The Empire of Lies: The Truth about China in the Twenty-first Century.* New York: Encounter Books, 2010.

Spencer, Jonathan. "Collective Violence and Everyday Practice in Sri Lanka." *Modern Asian Studies* 24, no. 3 (1990): 603–23.

Stafford, Charles. "The Discourse of Race in Modern China." *Man: The Journal of the Royal Anthropological Institute* 28, no. 3 (1993): 609.

Su, Xiaokang. "River Elegy." *Chinese Sociology and Anthropology* 24, no. 2 (1991–92): 7–18.

Sun Bin. *The Art of Warfare.* Translated by D. C. Lau and Roger T. Ames. Albany: State University of New York Press, 2003.

Sun, Lung-Kee. *The Chinese National Character: From Nationhood to Individuality.* New York: Routledge, 2002.

Sun Tzu. *The Art of Warfare.* Translated by Roger Ames. New York: Ballantine Books, 1993.

Sun Yat-sen. *Memoirs of a Chinese Revolutionary: A Programme of National Reconstruction for China.* Reprint, New York: AMS Press, 1970.

———. *The Three Principles of Democracy [San Min Chi I].* Translated by F. W. Price. Shanghai: Commercial Press, 1927.

———. *The Three Principles of the People [Sanminzhuyi].* Shanghai: Shangwu yinshuguan, 1927.

Suzuki, Shogo. "Why Does China Participate in Intrusive Peacekeeping? Understanding Paternalistic Chinese Discourses on Development and Intervention." *International Peacekeeping* 18, no. 3 (2011): 271–85.

Swaine, Michael D. "China's Assertive Behavior—Part Three: The Role of the Military in Foreign Policy." *China Leadership Monitor*, no. 36 (2012): 1–17.

———. "Xi Jinping's Trip to Latin America." *China Leadership Monitor*, no. 45 (2014): 1–23.

Synglobe. "Xi Jinping's Five Proposals for the Belt and Road Initiative," May 16, 2017. Available at https://synglobe.net/2017/05/16/xi-jinpings-five-proposals-for-the -belt- and-road-initiative/.

Tan, Alexander, and Boyu Chen. "China's Competing and Co-opting Nationalisms: Implications to Sino-Japanese Relations." *Pacific Focus*, 28, no. 3 (2013): 365–83.

Tang Wenfang, and Benjamin Darr. "Chinese Nationalism and Its Political and Social Origins." *Journal of Contemporary China* 21, no. 77 (2012): 811–26.

Taylor, Ian. *China's New Role in Africa.* Boulder: Lynne Rienner, 2009.

———. "China's Oil Diplomacy in Africa." *International Affairs* 82, no. 4 (2006): 937–59.

Teng, Ssu-yu, and John K. Fairbank. *China's Response to the West: A Documentary Survey, 1839–1923.* Cambridge: Harvard University Press, 1981.

Teufel-Dreyer, June. "Go West Young Han: The Hsia Fang Movement to China's Minority Areas." *Pacific Affairs* 48, no. 3 (1975): 353–69.

Thayer, Bradley A. "Humans, Not Angels: Considering the Decline of War Thesis." *International Studies Review* 15, no. 3 (2013): 405–11.

Toh Han Shih. *Is China an Empire?* Singapore: World Scientific, 2017.

Townsend, James. "Chinese Nationalism." *Australian Journal of Chinese Affairs*, no. 27 (1992): 97–130.

Tuttle, Gray. "China's Problem with Race: How Beijing Represses Minorities." *Foreign Affairs* 94, no. 3 (2015): 39–47.

Unger, Jonathan. *Chinese Nationalism.* Armonk NY: M. E. Sharpe, 1996.

U.S. Census Bureau. "Demographic Overview—Custom Region—China," data for 2012. Available at www.census.gov/population/international/data/idb/region.php.

van den Berghe, Pierre L. *The Ethnic Phenomenon.* Westport CT: Praeger, 1981.

Van Evera, Stephen. *Causes of War: Power and the Roots of Conflict.* Ithaca: Cornell University Press, 1999.

———. "Hypotheses on Nationalism and War." *International Security* 18, no. 4 (1994): 5–39.

———. "Primed for Peace: Europe after the Cold War." *International Security* 15, no. 3 (1990–91): 7–57.

Villard, Florent. "'Class,' 'Race,' and Language: Imagining China and the Discourse on the Category 'Han' in the Writing of Marxist Revolutionary Qu Qiubai (1899–1935)." *Asian Ethnicity* 11, no. 3 (2010): 311–24.

Wade, Abdoulaye. "Time for the West to Practise What It Preaches." *Financial Times,* January 24, 2008, 6.

Wade, Peter. "Racial Identity and Nationalism: A Theoretical View from Latin America." *Ethnic and Racial Studies* 24, no. 5 (2001): 845–65.

Waldron, Arthur. "The Art of *Shi*." *New Republic* 216, no. 25 (1997): 36–41.

———, ed. *China in Africa.* Washington DC: Jamestown Foundation, 2008.

Wang Gungwu, "Early Ming Relations with Southeast Asia: A Background Essay." In *The Chinese World Order: Traditional China's Foreign Relations,* edited by John K. Fairbank, 34–62. Cambridge: Harvard University Press, 1968.

Wang, Y. C. *Chinese Intellectuals and the West, 1872–1949.* Chapel Hill: University of North Carolina Press, 1966.

Wang, Yuan-Kang. *Harmony and War: Confucian Culture and Chinese Power Politics.* New York: Columbia University Press, 2011.

Wang, Zheng. "National Humiliation, History Education, and the Politics of Historical Memory: Patriotic Education Campaign in China." *International Studies Quarterly* 52, no. 4 (2008): 783–806.

———. *Never Forget National Humiliation: Historical Memory in Chinese Politics and Foreign Relations.* New York: Columbia University Press, 2012.

Weatherly, Robert. *Making China Strong: The Role of Nationalism in Chinese Thinking on Democracy and Human Rights.* New York: Palgrave Macmillan, 2014.

Weiss, Jessica Chen. "Authoritarian Signaling, Mass Audiences, and Nationalist Protest in China." *International Organization* 67, no. 1 (2013): 1–35.

———. "Popular Protest, Nationalism, and Domestic-International Linkages in Chinese Politics." In *Emerging Trends in the Social and Behavioral Sciences: An Interdisciplinary, Searchable, and Linkable Resource*, edited by Robert Scott and Stephen Kosslyn, 1–15. New York: Wiley, 2015.

———. *Powerful Patriots: Nationalist Protest in China's Foreign Relations.* Oxford: Oxford University Press, 2014.

Wertime, David, and Ning Hui. "Is This the New Face of China's Silent Majority?" *Foreign Policy*, October 22, 2014. Available at http://foreignpolicy.com/2014/10/22/is-this-the-new-face-of-chinas-silent-majority/.

Westad, Odd Arne. *Restless Empire: China and the World since 1750.* New York: Basic Books, 2012.

Whitmeyer, Joseph M. "Elites and Popular Nationalism." *British Journal of Sociology* 53, no. 3 (2002): 321–41.

"Wild West: Ethnic Tensions Remain High China's Xinjiang." *IHS Jane's Intelligence Review* 24, no. 8 (2012): 14–17.

Wimmer, Andreas. "Explaining Xenophobia and Racism: A Critical Review of Current Research Approaches." *Ethnic and Racial Studies* 20, no. 1 (1997): 17–41.

Wong, Edward. "In New China, 'Hostile' West Is Still Derided." *New York Times*, November 11, 2014. Available at http://www.nytimes.com/2014/11/12/world/asia/china-turns-up-the-rhetoric-against-the-west.html.

———. "Xi Again Defends China's Claim to the South China Sea Islands." *New York Times*, November 7, 2015. Available at http://www.nytimes.com/2015/11/08/world/asia/xi-jinping-china-south-china-sea-singapore.html.

Wong, Young-tsu. *Search for Modern Nationalism: Zhang Binglin and Revolutionary China, 1869–1936.* Oxford: Oxford University Press, 1989.

Woods, Jackson S., and Bruce J. Dickson. "Victims and Patriots: Disaggregating Nationalism in Urban China." *Journal of Contemporary China* 26, no. 104 (2017): 167–82.

Wu, Xu. *Chinese Cyber Nationalism: Evolution, Characteristics, and Implications.* Lanham MD: Lexington Books, 2007.

"Xi Stresses Continuation of Native Culture." *People's Daily Online*, September 24, 2014. Available at http://english.people.com.cn/n/2014/0924/c90785–8787237.html.

"Xinjiang: Fast and Loose." *Economist*, August 18, 2012, 39.

Xu, Ben. "Chinese Populist Nationalism: Its Intellectual Politics and Moral Dilemma." *Representations* 76, no. 1 (2001): 120–40.

Yahuda, Michael. "China's New Assertiveness in the South China Sea." *Journal of Contemporary China* 22, no. 81 (2013): 446–59.

Yan Xuetong. *Ancient Chinese Thought, Modern Chinese Power.* Translated by Edmund Ryden. Princeton: Princeton University Press, 2011.

Yang, Guobin. *The Power of the Internet in China: Citizen Activism Online.* New York: Columbia University Press, 2009.

———. "The Return of Ideology and the Future of Chinese Internet Policy." *Critical Studies in Mass Communication* 31, no. 2 (2014): 109–13.

Yang Haiyan. "Encountering Darwin and Creating Darwinism in China." In *The Cambridge Encyclopedia of Darwin and Evolutionary Thought*, edited by Michael Ruse, 250–57. Cambridge: Cambridge University Press, 2013.

Yang, Lijun, and Yongnian Zheng. "*Fen Qings* (Angry Youth) in Contemporary China." *Journal of Contemporary China* 21, no. 76 (2012): 637–53.

You Ji. "Nationalism, the Chinese Defence Culture, and the People's Liberation Army." In *Nationalism, Democracy, and National Integration in China*, edited by Liew and Shaoguang Wang, 247–60. New York: Routledge, 2004.

———. "The PLA and Diplomacy: Unraveling Myths about the Military Role in Foreign Policy Making." *Journal of Contemporary China* 23, no. 86 (2014): 236–54.

Yu, Haiyang. "Glorious Memories of Imperial China and the Rise of Chinese Populist Nationalism." *Journal of Contemporary China* 23, no. 90 (2014): 1174–87.

"Yuan Guiren: University Teachers Must Maintain Political, Legal, and Moral Bottom Lines" [袁贵仁:高校教师必须守好政治、法律、道德三条底线. *Xinhua Net*, January 29, 2015. Available at http://news.xinhuanet.com/2015–01/29/c_1114183715.htm.

Zarrow, Peter. *After Empire: The Conceptual Transformation of the Chinese State, 1885–1924.* Stanford: Stanford University Press, 2014.

———. "Historical Trauma: Anti-Manchuism and Memories of Atrocity in Late Qing China." *History and Memory* 16, no. 2 (2004): 67–107.

Zeng, Jinghan. *The Chinese Communist Party's Capacity to Rule: Ideology, Legitimacy and Party Cohesion.* New York: Palgrave Macmillan, 2016.

Zhang, Feng. "Chinese Exceptionalism in the Intellectual World of China's Foreign Policy." In *China across the Divide: The Domestic and Global in Politics and Society*, edited by Rosemary Foot, 43–71. Oxford: Oxford University Press, 2013.

———. "The Rise of Chinese Exceptionalism in International Relations." *European Journal of International Relations* 19, no. 2 (2011): 305–28.

Zhang Weiwei. *The China Wave: Rise of a Civilizational State.* Hackensack NJ: World Century, 2012.

Zhao, Dingxin. "Nationalism and Authoritarianism: Student-Government Conflicts during the 1999 Beijing Student Protests." *Asian Perspective* 27, no. 1 (2003): 5–34.

Zhao, Gang. "Reinventing China: Imperial Qing Ideology and the Rise of Modern Chinese National Identity in the Early Twentieth Century." *Modern China* 32, no. 1 (2006): 3–30.

Zhao, Suisheng. "China's Pragmatic Nationalism: Is It Manageable?" *Washington Quarterly* 29, no. 1 (2005): 131–44.

———. "Chinese Nationalism and Its International Orientations." *Political Science Quarterly* 15, no. 1 (2000): 1–33.

———. "Foreign Policy Implications of Chinese Nationalism Revisited: The Strident Turn." *Journal of Contemporary China* 22, no. 82 (2013): 535–53.

———. "A State-Led Nationalism: The Patriotic Education Campaign in Post-Tiananmen China." *Communist and Post-Communist Studies* 31, no. 3 (1998): 287–302.

Zhao, Yuezhi. *Communication in China: Political Economy, Power, and Conflict.* Lanham: Rowman and Littlefield, 2008.

Zhao, Zhenzhou, and Gerard A. Postiglione. "Representations of Ethnic Minorities in China's University Media." *Discourse* 21, no. 4 (2010): 1–18.

Zheng, Yongnian. *Discovering Chinese Nationalism in China: Modernization, Identity, and International Relations.* Cambridge: Cambridge University Press, 1999.

Zhongguo geming bowuguan [Revolutionary History Museum of China], ed. *Zhongguo: Cong quru zouxiang huihuang* [China: From humiliation to glory], *1840–1997*, vol. 1. Beijing: Chinese National Photography Press, 1997.

Zhou Xiaoping. "The Nine Knockout Blows in America's Cold War against China" [美国 对华文化冷战的九大绝招]. Available at http://news.sina.com.cn/zl/zatan /blog/2014-06-23/09331699/1218478775/48a082b70101i7j2.shtml.

Zou Rong [Tsou Jung]. *The Revolutionary Army: A Chinese Nationalist Tract of 1903.* Translated by John Lust. The Hague: Mouton, 1968.

INDEX

Page numbers with "t" indicate tables

Zhongguo wenming (Chinese civilization). *See* Chinese civilization *(Zhongguo wenming)*

zhongzu geming (racial revolution). *See* racial revolution *(minzu geming)*

Zhou Xiaoping, 47, 48, 49, 51–52

Zhuge Liang, 74

Zou Rong, 23, 25–26, 28–29, 31

zuguo ("ancestral nation" concept), 4, 14, 24